Prais

Image of th

'Amy is an expert storyteller, a well of emotion and reflection, and a follower of Jesus with a deep, genuine hunger for the reality of God. This fine book, helping us reach out to the Father, is filled with who she is.'
Adrian Plass, author and speaker

'Amy Scott Robinson's selection of daily readings and commentary makes for a powerful and transformative Advent journey. Taking the hardest little word of all, that word "God", a word that can be everything or nothing, a word that seems to carry no image with it and evades our understanding at every turn, Amy takes us on a journey through scripture in which she makes biblical image after image richly available to our imaginations so that we can come closer to God as he comes closer to us in Advent. I am particularly impressed by the way she thinks about the arts and engages the artistic imagination without ever losing the common touch or the simple but illuminating turn of phrase. Strongly recommended.'
Malcolm Guite, priest and poet

'Sometimes we need a poet's eye to see the God of the Bible afresh. Poet, storyteller and theologian Amy Scott Robinson uses the Bible's own metaphors of God as artisan, metalworker, consuming fire and others to lead us more deeply into our understanding of God. If you like C.S. Lewis, Malcolm Guite or Lauren Winner, you will love this outstanding book of thought-provoking, gasp-inducing, beautiful devotions to enrich your vision of God.'
Tanya Marlow, author of *Those Who Wait: Finding God in disappointment, doubt and delay*

'What a stunning gift this book is! Open it day by day as you ponder the God who reveals himself as a burning bush, weaver, gardener, shepherd, king, and, of course, baby. Amy Robinson helps us to unwrap the images of the invisible, the God who became flesh. Her book is a masterpiece of metaphor, a creative unlocking of what we might have missed. Through her creative, thought-provoking, deep and winsome writing, she leads us to the God who makes himself known.'
Amy Boucher Pye, author of *The Living Cross*

The Bible Reading Fellowship
15 The Chambers, Vineyard
Abingdon OX14 3FE
brf.org.uk

The Bible Reading Fellowship (BRF) is a Registered Charity (233280)

ISBN 978 0 85746 789 8
First published 2019
10 9 8 7 6 5 4 3 2 1 0
All rights reserved

Text © Amy Scott Robinson 2019
This edition © The Bible Reading Fellowship 2019
Cover image: wood engraving © Jonathan Gibbs

The author asserts the moral right to be identified as the author of this work

Acknowledgements
Unless otherwise acknowledged, scripture quotations are taken from The New
Revised Standard Version of the Bible, Anglicised edition, copyright © 1989, 1995 by
the Division of Christian Education of the National Council of the Churches of Christ
in the United States of America. Used by permission. All rights reserved.

Scripture quotations marked 'ESV' are taken from the Holy Bible, English Standard
Version, published by HarperCollins Publishers, © 2001 Crossway Bibles, a division
of Good News Publishers. Used by permission. All rights reserved.

Every effort has been made to trace and contact copyright owners for material used
in this resource. We apologise for any inadvertent omissions or errors, and would
ask those concerned to contact us so that full acknowledgement can be made in
the future.

A catalogue record for this book is available from the British Library

Printed and bound by CPI Group (UK) Ltd, Croydon CR0 4YY.

Image
of the Invisible

Daily Bible readings from
Advent to Epiphany

AMY SCOTT ROBINSON

For my husband Tiffer,
who checks my theology, laughs at my jokes
and keeps my teacup full.

Contents

Introduction

When you hear the name 'God', does an image come into your head? Do you think of him as a shining light, with a human shape, as an anchor in the storm, as a rock or as a fortress?

The Bible is full of metaphors for God, images that help us to experience a little of his character. Some of them are more familiar to us than others, perhaps because of well-known verses, songs or prayers in which God is named as a rock, a good shepherd or a king.

'Metaphor', from the Greek *meta* (between) and *phero* (I carry), literally means 'carrying across'. In fact, the word 'transfer' comes from exactly the same two words in Latin. So we can think of each of these biblical images as a way for our huge, inexplicable, incomprehensible God to be *carried across* to us, *transferred* from a heavenly truth to an earthly understanding. Each metaphor does this so that we can comprehend, encounter and worship God. The rich number of images means that we are able to keep meeting God, and praising him, in new ways throughout the seasons of our lives.

Metaphors for God respond to human need: sometimes we may greet him with joy like the morning star; at other times we may hide in him as our stronghold, run to him as our parent, feed on him as our bread. Since God is best described in relationship like this, each metaphor for God also has something to teach us about ourselves, our spiritual needs and how we can find those deep needs met in God. In every metaphor for God, we will find ourselves also pictured: as a baby bird hiding under its mother's wings, as people who are hungry or thirsty or stranded, or as someone waiting in darkness and longing for light. The better we know God in scripture, the better we see our own spiritual condition as well.

Very early on in the western church, before the sixth century, a tradition began of singing seven Advent prayers, one for each day of the week leading up to Christmas. These are known as the O Antiphons, and each one addresses the coming Christ directly, using one of the titles that come from the Old Testament: Wisdom, Adonai, Root of Jesse, Key of David, Rising Sun (or Morning Star, Dayspring), King of Nations and Emmanuel. These titles are linked to Old Testament prophetic metaphors that described the expected Messiah. Although the O Antiphons are seldom chanted in churches now, they survive in the familiar Advent carol 'O Come, O Come, Emmanuel'.

The O Antiphons imaginatively link us to the people who were waiting for the first coming of Christ, needing the Messiah they had been promised. The images offer us metaphors not only for God but also for humanity without God: people in need of wisdom, a king, a key.

This book, leaning in to the tradition of the Advent antiphons, offers a selection of metaphors for God, not just for the final seven days but for every day of Advent and all twelve days of Christmas, finishing with Epiphany on 6 January. I would like to invite you to explore them all and to pray with me, addressing God with all these different names, so that we can wonder all the more richly at the incarnation: the fact that, in Jesus, we have the 'image of the invisible God' (Colossians 1:15), God with us on earth. In Jesus, at Christmas, the waiting was over and all the needs and hopes named in the antiphons were fulfilled.

Week I

WHEN GOD APPEARS

Many of the metaphors in this book come from the inspired poetry and prophecy of the Old Testament writers. Some of them come from the mouth of Jesus himself, from his 'I am' sayings and parables. Most of them are metaphors in the sense of being a comparison, an invitation to 'think of it like this', a tangible object or image to help us grasp one aspect of an intangible God.

However, we are beginning this journey by exploring metaphor in its literal sense of something being carried across, so we will look at some of the different ways in which God carried himself across to communicate with his people during the time of the Old Testament. These stories are remarkable, because God, who is everywhere and eternal, found a way to also be in one place and at one time in history.

In these stories of Moses and Elijah, Joshua and Hagar, we can see what happens when God appears and how he is directly experienced by his people. How did God choose to represent himself to them, and what might those images mean for us today?

1 December

The burning bush

Exodus 3:1-3

> Moses was keeping the flock of his father-in-law Jethro, the priest of Midian; he led his flock beyond the wilderness, and came to Horeb, the mountain of God. There the angel of the Lord appeared to him in a flame of fire out of a bush; he looked, and the bush was blazing, yet it was not consumed. Then Moses said, 'I must turn aside and look at this great sight, and see why the bush is not burned up.'

Once upon a time, a murderer was sitting up a mountain looking after his father-in-law's sheep. At the top of the mountain, he had reached the bottom of himself. Brought up as an Egyptian even though he was born a Hebrew, he had spent his childhood being served by his own people as slaves while he lived uneasily in the palace. Eventually, in his confusion and anger, he had killed an Egyptian slave driver.

He had only tried to be a go-between, a peacekeeper, as he always had, and he didn't learn from the experience. After the murder, he confronted two squabbling Hebrews and tried to solve their quarrel. When they reacted angrily, showing that they knew what he had done to the Egyptian, he ran away. He met his Midianite wife when he rescued her and her sisters from shepherds who were trying to drive them away from a well: the go-between yet again.

Stretched between three peoples, his name meant 'pulled out' and that's just how he felt: pulled out of an identity, pulled in all directions, pulled out of society and community and humanity, sitting there with someone else's sheep. He was a failed peacemaker, a go-between who had been squeezed out, belonging nowhere. Then he looked up and saw a bush on fire.

Except the bush was not really on fire. It was more that the fire was on the bush; the bush itself was not burning up. And then a voice spoke from it, and history changed forever. The go-between was chosen to go between God and his people. Old Pulled Out ended up pulling God's people out of slavery, parting the sea, receiving the ten commandments and leading Israel through the wilderness until, from the top of another mountain, he glimpsed the promised land.

In this first encounter with Moses, God carries himself across in a number of important ways. He shows himself as a great and holy God: Moses has to take off his shoes to stand on such sacred ground. He demonstrates that he is a God of miracles and power: in their ensuing conversation, Moses witnesses his staff turning into a snake and back, as well as himself both developing and being healed from leprosy in record time. God names himself as Yahweh, 'I Am', an awesome, unquestionable and all-encompassing name. He also uses an image: God represents himself to Moses by showing him a fire on a bush.

The image piques Moses' curiosity; he says, 'I must turn aside and look at this great sight.' But perhaps there is more to it than that. As we will see, elsewhere God appears as a consuming fire, coming out of nowhere in power to accept a sacrifice, his holiness represented in unbearable heat and flame. Here, though, the fire that should destroy the bush does not consume it, and the God who should be too holy to approach does not destroy Moses, the runaway murderer. Moses must take off his shoes, but beyond that he does not behave like somebody face-to-face with a holy and powerful God. In fact, Moses argues with him. He disagrees and refuses and makes excuses, and still Yahweh does not destroy him or even give up and choose someone else.

There is an unusual grace in the burning bush, because it is an image of pure light and holiness that does not destroy. The bush is transfigured with holy fire, but it is unharmed; it's still the same bush underneath, rooted where it was before, its randomly seeded place on the mountainside accidentally making it a megaphone for God's voice.

The burning bush sets a theme for Moses' relationship with God from then on, because as the go-between Moses will become a megaphone too. Moses, the same Moses with his roots exactly where they needed to be in both the Egyptian palace and his Hebrew family, will need to veil his face because it shines with God. His encounters with God will transfigure but not destroy him.

The burning bush offers an image for the future of Israel too, as they encounter God's anger alongside his mercy and grace. They will spend 40 years in the wilderness with God but emerge unharmed: still Israel, still God's people, still heading for the land he promised them. Over and over again, Moses will be the one standing between God's fury and God's people. Moses will be the only one allowed to talk back, to plead, to argue. He will carry across the complaints of the people to God, and he will carry God's instructions and mercy back to the people. The whole relationship of God with Israel will be based on justice and mercy: the justice of fire that is meant to consume and the mercy of the bush remaining unharmed.

It's a fitting beginning to a collection of metaphors for God. In every image, we will see the holy and omnipresent God revealed in a particular earthly object. The presence of God, even as a comparison, transfigures the object and makes it shine with holiness, so that in a bird or a seed or a door we can momentarily glimpse the divine. These things are still themselves, and we are still ourselves, but God has allowed us to experience his holiness and remain unharmed. Unharmed, but not, perhaps, unchanged.

A suggestion

Today, look out for the holy in the ordinary. Where can you see glimpses of light, hints of God, in your encounters or in everyday objects? Where do you find examples of grace, of mercy? Watch for the moment when you can turn aside, get a little closer and find yourself on holy ground.

A prayer to God in the burning bush

Lord, you are holy, unnameable, indescribable light and power. Yet in your mercy you have invited me to come closer, to hear you, even to answer you. I am standing on holy ground, but the sight of you beckons me. Speak, Lord, even hard things: I will try to listen, try to follow.

2 December

Pillars of cloud and fire

Exodus 13:21-22

> The Lord went in front of them in a pillar of cloud by day, to lead them along the way, and in a pillar of fire by night, to give them light, so that they might travel by day and by night. Neither the pillar of cloud by day nor the pillar of fire by night left its place in front of the people.

A few days ago, I was on a train that I think may have crossed into another dimension. Here's what happened: we were rattling along in wintery sunshine, listening to the announcements giving familiar excuses about why this train would be delayed, when I looked out of the window and saw a magnificent double rainbow just ahead of us. The end of the rainbow started in the field to our right and arched up and over the railway track, so that it looked like a bridge deliberately placed for the train to travel right underneath it. This sight stayed ahead of us for about ten minutes, the rainbow always seeming to start at the far edge of the next field along. But then the train really did seem to enter the rainbow, because suddenly everything was bathed in that golden autumnal light that makes the trees look as if they are carved out of precious metals. At this point I checked my ticket to make sure that we were still heading for Norwich rather than Fairyland, but when I next looked up there was something else ahead of us: deep grey and purple cloud. We had travelled into a rainstorm. Everything continued to look like Tiffany stained glass for another minute, and then the first drops spattered on the window pane; we left the Elysian fields behind us and continued on our journey to Norfolk.

As the sky changed back to bleak and boring, I wondered what God must have looked like when he went ahead of the Israelites in the wilderness inside a weather system. All Exodus tells us is that God was in a pillar of cloud by day. Do you imagine it as white, grey, purple or shot through with rainbow colours? Angry like a thundercloud or shining with a sunburst?

God's appearance as cloud and fire to guide his people shows him as mysterious, unknowable. If the Lord was in the pillar of cloud, he remained unseen. When we lose our way, we sometimes describe life as foggy or clouded, but here God is giving clear guidance from inside the fog. He uses the cloud, the very thing that hides him, to lead the way and make his direction clear.

The cloud is always ahead of the Israelites. Just as a rainbow always seems to begin in the next field along as you approach it, God is leading them and is with them, but they can never get closer to him. There's a constant distance in their relationship. He is there and not there, like mist, like a cloud.

Then, at night, the guidance system changes to become a pillar of fire, and the description in Exodus adds 'to give them light'. Now God is not only guiding, but also acting as a lamp to light their way. I wonder how quickly the cloud transformed into fire as the sun went down. Exodus doesn't say, but I imagine that the darker it got, the brighter God shone for his wandering people. The psalmist says: 'Even the darkness is not dark to you; the night is as bright as the day, for darkness is as light to you' (Psalm 139:12).

The God in the pillar of cloud and fire is brighter in our darkness, more visible and present the harder things get. This is reflected in human nature: it's in the worst moments of life that people report sending up desperate prayers. The tougher life is, the more urgently we look for a reason, a hope and a guide. It's in those moments that we may fix our eyes on God as a beacon. He may still seem distant, still moving away ahead of us, but at least he is visible, giving light enough to lead us.

Finally, and most touchingly, the writer of Exodus points out, 'Neither the pillar of cloud by day nor the pillar of fire by night left its place in front of the people' (v. 22). These images in which God revealed himself to Israel may have held impressions of mystery, holiness, even distance; but the main impression was constancy. God might sometimes guide us from inside a fog of uncertainty or through our desperate need for light in dark times, but he does not depart from his purpose: to lead us until we find our rest in him.

A question

What about these images of God most attracts you: a guiding cloud up ahead, a light in darkness, a constant companion? Is it something that is true for you or something that you long for?

A prayer to God in pillars of cloud and fire

Guiding God, go before me every day and keep my eyes fixed on you. You are my clear way in times of uncertainty, you light my road in times of deep darkness, you fill the air with coloured light in times of joy. I praise you for your constant faithfulness.

3 December

Glorious presence

Exodus 33:18–23

> Moses said, 'Show me your glory, I pray.' And he said, 'I will
> make all my goodness pass before you, and will proclaim
> before you the name, "The Lord"; and I will be gracious to
> whom I will be gracious, and will show mercy on whom I will
> show mercy. But,' he said, 'you cannot see my face; for no one
> shall see me and live.' And the Lord continued, 'See, there is a
> place by me where you shall stand on the rock; and while my
> glory passes by I will put you in a cleft of the rock, and I will
> cover you with my hand until I have passed by; then I will take
> away my hand, and you shall see my back; but my face shall
> not be seen.'

We have accidental guinea pigs. We were given a pair to look after
for a while, and they stuck around and somehow became ours. What
we didn't realise at the time is that this means we will have guinea
pigs forever, because apparently if one of a pair dies, you have to
get a companion for the remaining guinea pig or it will pine away.
(In Switzerland, it's actually illegal to keep only one guinea pig.)
However, if you get another one the same age and size, the two
of them will fight. In order to make it obvious which guinea pig is
the leader, you have to get a smaller, younger pig than the one you
already have. That's how baby Bobby came into our home.

A baby guinea pig is a very fragile creature. Unused to being caught
and handled, and away from his mother for the first time, Bobby
arrived in a state of terror, and approaching him too quickly held a
real risk of a tiny cavy heart attack. To get him used to me, I gave

him a little hut to hide in and then sat with him in the pen and kept completely still while he built up the confidence to breathe, or even twitch, in my presence. Without the hiding place, an encounter with me really could have killed him.

In today's passage, Moses asks God, 'Show me your glory,' and God has to explain that to do so would kill Moses. God's glory is simply too awesome, too terrifying for the human frame to withstand the experience of seeing his face. But Moses has asked God to show him his ways, 'that I may know you and find favour in your sight' (v. 13). It's extraordinary that the man who, by this point, has been called by the burning bush, followed God's instruction through the ten plagues and parted the sea, struck water from a rock, was fed by manna, led by pillars of cloud and fire, and received the ten commandments still thinks that he doesn't 'know' God or God's ways. But Moses is aware of that distance, of God's greatness and his own smallness. He knows that there is far more to see and know, and so, even while he is in the sort of conversation with God that only a handful of people in history have ever experienced, he asks to get to know him better.

God's solution is to provide a hiding place so that Moses can have a glimpse of the sight that terrifies to the point of death. He will sit Moses in a crevice in the rock and then pass before him in glory, but he will cover Moses up with his hand so that he doesn't get to see the approach of God, only the retreat.

This new way of God's revealing himself to Moses may be more impressive, more awe-inspiring, perhaps even more personal and unique to Moses than any previously, but it certainly isn't more intimate. In fact, Moses' request to know God better has only resulted in a demonstration of how immensely unknowable by humans God really is. However, God is not doing things this way to prove a point, but to respond to Moses' request; there's a tenderness in the way he covers Moses with his hand as he passes, so that his face is hidden, which makes me wonder how God felt in that moment and whether God, as much as Moses, longed for more. We know that

God is incorporeal and doesn't have a hand or a face, other than metaphorically, and yet here is God in his fullest imaginable glory still communicating to Moses in human terms.

As I sat in Bobby's pen, waiting for him to poke his nose out of his little hut, I would have loved to scoop him up for a cuddle, but I knew that the time wasn't right for that yet. With persistence, though, and plenty of carrots as encouragement, the time would come. When God told Moses that he would cover him up with his hand and hide his face, perhaps he was thinking of the moment when he would have hands and a face and when he would reveal some of his dazzling glory to his disciples on a mountaintop; in that moment he would talk with Moses again and at last would be known face-to-face.

A suggestion

On one side of a sheet of paper, write down things that make you feel safe. On the other side, write the things that most terrify you. Which list is the best fit for God?

A prayer to God in glory

Lord, sometimes the thought of you is too awe-inspiring, too terrifying, simply too huge for me to contemplate. There are single stars in the universe you created that are bigger and brighter than I can imagine or describe, and you must be so much bigger, brighter and holier than they are! I long to know you better all the same, and I praise you for your promises that you have made that possible.

4 December
Consuming fire

1 Kings 18:37–38

> 'Answer me, O Lord, answer me, so that this people may know that you, O Lord, are God, and that you have turned their hearts back.' Then the fire of the Lord fell and consumed the burnt-offering, the wood, the stones, and the dust, and even licked up the water that was in the trench.

As I write, we've been seeing horrifying news of wildfires sweeping through California. Entire towns have been reduced to grey ash, in which you can only just make out the shapes of the foundations of buildings and where the roads used to be. One report said that the fire moved so fast it destroyed the equivalent of a football field every second. 'Not a single thing has been saved. It's all gone,' said a homeowner in an interview, standing in the space where his house had been.

For God to show himself as a consuming fire, then, is a terrifying prospect. Heat, destruction and speed: are these things we ever dare to associate with God? Elijah's expectation, though, is that this appearance would be impressive and incredibly powerful. His confidence in this is such that, in a land of extreme drought, he found gallons of water with which to soak the altar and the sacrifice and even create a little moat around it. When the fire falls, it consumes not just the offering but also the wood it is on, the stones of the altar, the dust of the ground and all the water. Not a single thing is left.

Quite apart from being an astonishing spectacle, this fire is also unmistakably from God. The people react by falling on their faces and repeating, 'The Lord indeed is God; the Lord indeed is God.' A similar thing happened to Gideon, when his visitor told him to pour broth over meat and unleavened bread, and fire came to consume the whole soggy concoction. 'Help me, Lord God! For I have seen the angel of the Lord face to face,' cried Gideon, assuming that he was going to die (Judges 6:20–23). The appearance of the fire, like Moses' burning bush, created holy ground: it brought the onlookers into the presence of God, at which point they knew they were in trouble and couldn't help but worship or, in the case of Gideon, panic.

Consuming fire was more recognisably divine to Elijah and Gideon than it is to our collective imagination today; in fact, we tend to shy away from such images that represent God as violent and devastating. Perhaps we are careful around images of fire because we want to avoid a certain stereotypical view of Christian preaching; or perhaps it's because of our own fear. I don't know about you, but there are many friendlier, cuddlier images of God in this book that I'm more comfortable interacting with than this one. However, it's worth being familiar with Elijah's expectation of power and Gideon's expectation of death on encountering God. The incarnation becomes all the more remarkable when we remember that when God reached down to earth, people used to recognise him when things caught fire; when God interacted with humanity, the assumption was that humanity's tiny offerings would be consumed and nothing would be left. Yet this is the same God who later made a little fire on a beach to cook some fish for breakfast; the same God who once took a small offering of five loaves and handed them out to a crowd until twelve baskets of food were left over. Instead of a paltry offering being consumed, everyone was fed. This Advent, let's allow those things to astonish us again.

A question

When have you been most convinced of the presence of God?

A prayer to God the consuming fire

The Lord indeed is God; the Lord indeed is God!

5 December

Silence

1 Kings 19:11–13

> He said, 'Go out and stand on the mountain before the Lord, for the Lord is about to pass by.' Now there was a great wind, so strong that it was splitting mountains and breaking rocks in pieces before the Lord, but the Lord was not in the wind; and after the wind an earthquake, but the Lord was not in the earthquake; and after the earthquake a fire, but the Lord was not in the fire; and after the fire a sound of sheer silence. When Elijah heard it, he wrapped his face in his mantle and went out and stood at the entrance of the cave. Then there came a voice to him that said, 'What are you doing here, Elijah?'

In the days when I still counted as 'youth', I loved to make a regular pilgrimage to Taizé. It's an ecumenical community in Burgundy, France, where about 100 brothers welcome thousands of young people from all over Europe and beyond. It's an extraordinary place where, as a visitor, you can put up a tent and spend a week or so sharing in the simple life, food, work and prayer of the brothers, as well as meeting all sorts of fascinating people from other countries and denominations on the same adventure of faith.

Three times a day, the Taizé bells ring to invite people to prayer. In a church whose walls can open out to accommodate 5,000 worshippers, the pilgrims gather for a service of basic chants – mainly verses of scripture in various languages so that everyone can join in – and silence. The chanted prayer builds to a silence lasting about ten minutes, and there is nothing on earth quite like the sound of 5,000 people all being absolutely quiet together.

There's an apocryphal story told by some of the Taizé brothers of a woman who came straight into the time of prayer when she first arrived and hadn't been warned about the silence. After a few confused minutes she leaned across to the brother praying next to her and asked, 'What are we waiting for?' He pondered this for a moment, and then whispered back, 'The kingdom of God.'

In this passage, up the mountain Elijah is waiting for God. The interesting thing is that he is not waiting for God in quite the same way we do. He is not waiting out of years of silence, out of doubt or because he lacks guidance. He is not waiting for a hidden, forgotten God or for a God whom he has never really seen act. On the contrary: not so long ago he witnessed God's fire appearing in power and consuming the altar along with the sacrifice. God has fed Elijah in the wilderness by sending ravens to him with bread. God has performed miracles for him by multiplying a widow's oil and flour to make daily food during the famine. God has even raised the same widow's son from the dead.

With all this in his recent past, Elijah is still waiting for God. He has positioned himself in a cave up a mountain, in the same hiding place on the same mountain from which Moses had been allowed to witness God's glory retreating, and perhaps he is thinking of that story as he waits. Even while he is waiting, God speaks to him and asks him what he's doing there, and Elijah replies with a list of all he's done for God, despite which his life is still in danger. He is talking with God, but still waiting for him, because it's not God's voice that he is waiting for; it's God himself.

I wonder whether Elijah, like Moses before him, is simply longing to know God more intimately in this moment. Has the awesome and terrifying display of fire actually put a little distance between God and his prophet? Or is it that, in the same situation as Moses was, feeling like the only one left while the whole of Israel has once again forsaken God, Elijah thinks that the logical next step is to go where Moses was and wait to be blessed in exactly the same way that Moses was?

Whatever Elijah is waiting for, God responds instead with what he actually needs. First, though, to drive the point home, God offers three displays of power and doesn't show up in any of them. Wind, earthquake and fire may be the kinds of displays that the prophets of Baal might have expected to represent a deity, but unlike the consuming fire in which God was instantly recognisable, it's also possible for him not to be involved with any of those things. Finally he shows Elijah something far more real: a low whisper, a light breeze or, as the NRSV tantalisingly translates it, 'a sound of sheer silence' (v. 12). At that point, Elijah wraps his face in his cloak and comes out of the cave, knowing that his wait is over.

Strangely, Elijah and God then have exactly the same conversation they had a few moments ago, but this time, I imagine, in a very different tone of voice. After that, it's back to work for Elijah: another wilderness to walk through, two kings and a prophet to anoint.

I don't know about you, but silence is a precious commodity for me these days, especially given that whenever it takes me by surprise, I am apt to fill it straight away with my phone or my work or by binge-watching sitcoms online. If you find yourself in silence at some point today, take a moment to listen to it. The God who is silence does not answer all our questions. He does not instantly solve all our problems or change our direction to something new and exciting. He does not come as we're expecting. He does not give us what we're looking for. He gives us what we need.

A suggestion

If you come across a moment of silence today, do not reach for your phone or make a coffee. Stop, wait and listen.

A prayer to God in silence

Lord, sometimes when I most wish you would act, when I'm looking out for a display of your power and glory, you arrive in sheer silence. Help me not to miss it. Come very close to me in those times. You know best what I need.

6 December

The angel of the Lord

Genesis 16:7–10, 13

> The angel of the Lord found her by a spring of water in the wilderness, the spring on the way to Shur. And he said, 'Hagar, slave-girl of Sarai, where have you come from and where are you going?' She said, 'I am running away from my mistress Sarai.' The angel of the Lord said to her, 'Return to your mistress, and submit to her.' The angel of the Lord also said to her, 'I will so greatly multiply your offspring that they cannot be counted for multitude'... So she named the Lord who spoke to her, 'You are El-roi'; for she said, 'Have I really seen God and remained alive after seeing him?'

Hagar crouched, exhausted, next to the spring of water and placed a hand on the little bump where her baby was growing. Perhaps she shouldn't have been so openly delighted when it had first started to show. She certainly shouldn't have assumed that her mistress would be happy for her, despite the fact that the whole thing had been Sarai's idea in the first place. Perhaps Hagar had been wrong about her position in the household now that she was pregnant with Abram's firstborn. After Sarai's cruel treatment, which was fuelled by grief and jealousy, Hagar had fled and was now in the wilderness, with nowhere to go. As she waited there, catching her breath, the angel of the Lord crouched down beside her.

Gideon, the youngest son in the weakest clan in Manasseh, was beating wheat in the winepress in the hope that those bullying Midianites might not see him and come and take the wheat away, as they had done to most of the rest of Israel's crops, flocks and possessions. Every now and then he looked nervously over his shoulder or peeped up above the rim of the winepress to scan the horizon for bands of marauders. That's why it nearly gave him a heart attack when he saw someone perched on the edge of the winepress. He hadn't seen or heard them approach. The angel of the Lord, without a hint of irony, greeted Gideon as a 'mighty man of valour' (Judges 6:12, ESV) even while he was still pressing himself, wide-eyed, against the wall.

Jacob was stuck between two grim-looking possibilities. Behind him was his father-in-law Laban, who now knew the full extent of Jacob's trickery and theft and who had set up a boundary marker so that the two of them would never again have to go near one another. Ahead of Jacob was his brother Esau, whom he had tricked out of a birthright and had not seen since. With him were his precious sons and daughters and both his wives. So Jacob sent his family ahead to a place of relative safety, and he stayed by the stream, pacing the ground and agonising. A man stepped out of the darkness and, without a word, engaged Jacob in a wrestling match until dawn, at which point he refused to give his name, because Jacob knew perfectly well who he was. 'I have seen God face to face, and yet my life is preserved,' said Jacob (Genesis 32:30).

Sometimes, the God of the Old Testament, the God of fire and cloud and sheer terrifying presence, needed to turn up with a more human shape. 'Angel' literally means 'messenger', but these encounters are with more than just a messenger sent from God. Hagar, Gideon, Jacob and several more in the Old Testament acknowledge that somehow, the person they have just seen and spoken with is God himself, God in the guise of a stranger. Some Bible scholars say that these appearances are the second person of the Trinity, Christ in a pre-incarnate form.

The people in these encounters acknowledge that they have seen God, but Hagar also calls him El-Roi, 'The God who sees', and in each situation that would be an apt name. The angel of the Lord meets people wherever they are – in hiding, in fear and in distress, apart from other people. He sees and provides exactly what is needed: encouragement for Hagar, a challenge for Gideon, a wrestling match and a new name for Jacob, a covenant for Abram, a refreshing dinner and drink for Elijah, protection from the furnace for Shadrach, Meshach and Abednego. He comes as a visitor, a stranger, who by the end of the encounter is both revealed as God and as an intimate friend. He is the God who sees and is seen.

A question

If the angel of the Lord were to turn up for you today, where would he find you? What situation would he see? Knowing that God sees you in that place, what can you say to him about it, and what would you love to hear in reply?

A prayer to God the stranger

Lord, I don't always recognise you, but you always see me. You know my most secret needs, and when I think I am hidden you are there with me. Today I pray that you will give me exactly the word, the encounter, the gift that I need to carry on, even if I only see your hand in it after the moment has passed.

7 December

The ark of the covenant

Joshua 8:33

> **All Israel, alien as well as citizen, with their elders and officers and their judges, stood on opposite sides of the ark in front of the levitical priests who carried the ark of the covenant of the Lord, half of them in front of Mount Gerizim and half of them in front of Mount Ebal, as Moses the servant of the Lord had commanded at the first, that they should bless the people of Israel.**

Joshua stood back and surveyed the finished altar. Not a single stone had been cut or shaped, just as Moses had commanded when he wrote his careful instructions for this moment of entrance into the promised land (Deuteronomy 27). This ceremony, the reading of the law and the blessings and curses, should be full of praise, triumph and celebration; but Joshua knew now how important the reading of the law was going to be, because already, in this new land, the law had been broken. Already they had suffered defeat at Ai and nearly lost everything because somebody had seen fit to turn their back on God, steal some plunder and then lie about it. Joshua sighed and ran a hand through his hair. These disobedient, wayward people, who had struggled so hard against God and Moses, were his problem now.

The crowd was beginning to gather. Joshua turned to the priests who were carrying the ark of the covenant. The ark, containing the ten commandments, a bowl of manna and Aaron's blossoming staff for remembrance, would represent God's witness to this renewal of their covenant. Nobody was in any doubt that God travelled with the ark. Ever since Moses had been given its exact dimensions by God, the ark had been with them, going before them, the place of communication between God and Israel. When the priests had walked into the Jordan with the ark, the waters had rushed backwards and let everyone pass on dry land; only once they had stepped back on to the bank did the river gush back into its bed. The ark had led the people around the city of Jericho, and the walls had fallen on the seventh turn. The ark itself was not God, but it was God's chosen seat because it contained God's word. It carried God across to the people. Joshua still felt his heart beat faster to see it approaching, this faithful, travelling holy place.

The contents of the ark were both a description of God and an instruction to be followed: it contained the word and the bread. Moses' instructions told them to eat together in this moment of arrival and to read the law. That was their worship, their closeness to the Lord: words and food. With the people gathered, and in sight of the ark of the covenant, Joshua began to write on the plastered stones. Once he had written out every word of the law, he stood back and read it in full, all the blessings and curses, so that everybody could hear: men, women and children, even the people who were not Israelites but had joined them along the way. This, he explained, is our God.

From that moment, through the ark's long history – through its being stolen and recovered and brought into Jerusalem with David singing and dancing, through its residence in the holy of holies in Solomon's temple and until it was either captured or hidden and forgotten in the exile to Babylon – God chose it as the place to represent him. It was a symbol containing symbols, a selection of metaphors: God could be met in the holy place, the mercy seat, between the gold cherubim on the top of the ark itself; the word represented in the ten commandments; the bread of heaven, God's provision, represented in the bowl of manna; and Aaron's staff like a flowering branch. We will meet each of them again, in some form, in this book as we explore the many ways, before and since, in which God has been carried across to his people.

Are there symbols or places that help to carry God across to you –
times or actions that feel particularly holy? Perhaps you light a
candle, use a holding cross or cherish the moment of taking the
Communion cup. The importance Joshua placed on the ark of the
covenant can reassure us that, although no one thing can contain or
define God, symbols can be a valuable meeting place and a real help
to our worship and prayer.

A suggestion

Draw a large box. Inside it, draw (or write, if you prefer) the things
you would put inside your own ark. These could be things, like
the manna, that represent your own memories of when God has
provided for you or when you have encountered him. They could be
things, like the tablets of the law, that have always helped you into
prayer and spiritual life: special verses, places, symbols. Keep your
box near you when you pray this week.

A prayer to God in symbol

Father, you made us with senses and gave us things that delight
them. You designed each of us so that certain colours, music
or textures can rouse us or calm us. Sometimes, certain things
or places give me such a sense of your presence that they are
a way of anchoring me to you, especially in times when I am
busy or struggling to pray. Thank you for those blessings. I know
that you are everywhere, but it's good to have a meeting place
where I can seek you out.

At the end of week I

- Do any of the images of God we have encountered so far feel familiar to you? Which ones feel more distant or foreign?

- Which of the images or stories stick in your mind more than others?

- If you could encounter God in one of the ways described in this chapter, which would you choose – or would you choose none of the above? Why?

- If Moses, Elijah or Abraham had been told that God would one day walk on the earth as a human being, what kind of person do you think they would have imagined?

Week 2

GOD THE CREATOR

We recognise God as the creator of the world, the universe and everything in it, but God's creative traits are not limited to the first chapters of Genesis. In all of this week's readings, God is described as a creator of smaller things, engaged in specific crafts. These metaphors show us a creative, skilled God, working diligently and imaginatively in an artistic discipline. We can imagine him in his workshop, with a honed knowledge of his craft.

It's interesting to put an omniscient, eternal God into this framework, because we know the creative process to be one of trial and error and happy mistakes, and we're used to the thing we create never quite being the same as the thing we imagined when we began. When God is referred to as a potter or a weaver, we have to wonder what these time-bound, error-filled processes can possibly tell us about a perfect creator God.

All these images are double metaphors, because if God is the creator, then we, his creations, are represented by the art he is making. If God is a potter, we are clay; if God is a weaver, we are the fabric on the loom. This week, we can consider what it might mean for us to be these objects in the hands of God and how it feels to be half-made, unfinished works of art whose end has already been imagined by the artist.

These are rich metaphors, which give rise to themes of God's planning, forethought and imagination as well as our own mortality, mutability and purpose. Yet part of the purpose of most art is to be beautiful, and artists take delight in their creations and enjoy their work, meaning that these images are also a set of descriptions of a close and tender relationship between God and his people.

8 December

Poet

John 1:1–4

In the beginning was the Word, and the Word was with God, and the Word was God. He was in the beginning with God. All things came into being through him, and without him not one thing came into being. What has come into being in him was life, and the life was the light of all people.

Words are twisty, fidgety, flickering little things. As a writer, I know this well. Words fascinate me deeply, but sometimes they run away with me. Or from me. Sometimes they run out altogether.

Watch a child learning to talk and you may glimpse that moment of excitement when they first discover that speaking a word like 'biscuit' or 'drink' can get them the thing itself. The word 'biscuit' is not a biscuit, but magically it represents one enough to produce something sweet, crunchy and edible.

The next thing you might notice is the frustration and confusion when the child says 'biscuit' again the next day and is given a custard cream where previously the same word produced a bourbon. Words represent slightly different things to different people. The need of a child to develop extra language in order to ask for the things she wants is the same need that hits a poet, chewing the end of her pencil and wondering exactly how to describe the sunset she's looking at so that other readers will understand that precise shade of deep purple and its contrast to that dying burnt orange.

Every single word we use is a tiny metaphor. It only represents the thing we are talking about. But when God uses a word, it results in the thing. God's word is creation. He says, 'Let there be light', and the thing he is imagining becomes reality (Genesis 1:3). He says, 'Let the waters under the sky be gathered together into one place, and let the dry land appear' (Genesis 1:9), and creation obeys. Not only does creation obey God's words, but it does so with a kind of echo of them, so that 'the heavens are telling the glory of God' (Psalm 19:1); the psalmist creates an image of the sky full of speech and words that can be heard everywhere, in every language: 'Their voice goes out through all the earth, and their words to the end of the world' (Psalm 19:4).

Studying English at university, we discussed lots of different definitions of poetry. My favourite was Tom Stoppard's: 'Poetry is the simultaneous compression of language and expansion of meaning.' In other words, the fewer words you can use and the greater meaning you can express with them, the closer you are to a perfect poem. God said, 'Let there be light.' In Hebrew, that's two words. What a poem!

Another definition came from Samuel Taylor Coleridge, who defined prose as 'words in their best order' and poetry as 'the best words in the best order'. Poets do their best to hone and define their word choices so that they are able to conjure up images, creating little worlds in the imaginations of their readers. God, the ultimate poet, uses word and order perfectly enough to create everything.

The apostle Paul writes, 'For we are his workmanship, created in Christ Jesus for good works' (Ephesians 2:10, ESV). The word translated 'workmanship' is the Greek *poema*. While it is the root of our word 'poem', that's not what it actually meant in Greek; it would be wrong to translate it as saying that we are 'God's poem', since the word was not used in that way until centuries later and in a different language! On the other hand, the whole of creation is God's spoken word in living form. Everything appeared through God's words. Everything is God's poem.

The writer of Psalm 19, of course, like John writing the prologue to his gospel, is a poet attempting to line up his own little words in the right order to describe the Word. No wonder he finishes his psalm with the prayer, 'Let the words of my mouth… be acceptable to you, O Lord' (Psalm 19:14). Human words can only go so far to explain God, but as Christians, we believe that the Word became flesh. Jesus is the image of the invisible God, because as the Word himself, he is not just a description, not just a metaphor. He is Emmanuel – God with us.

A suggestion

Pay close attention to the words around you today, both spoken and written, by you and by others. How effective are they? How powerful? How creative? Does focusing on them make you want to change any of them? In what way?

A prayer to God the poet

Lord, thank you for words, for their power to move and entertain us. Help me to hear the words you have for me today, and, in every encounter, may all the words I use today chime with your living Word.

9 December

Musician

Zephaniah 3:17

> The Lord, your God, is in your midst,
>   a warrior who gives victory;
> he will rejoice over you with gladness,
>   he will renew you in his love;
> he will exult over you with loud singing.

I grew up surrounded by singing. My mother is brilliantly able to make up a tune to any poem she finds in a book; household appliances and cleaning fluids also had their own theme tunes as I toddled about after her, 'helping' with the housework. Visiting my grandparents, it was clear where she'd got it from. Grandma was an entertaining jazz pianist, and I remember my grandfather singing to me, bouncing me along with the rhythm of 'This is the way the ladies ride' until that moment when the rider falls off, and I would be 'dropped' and caught, giggling hysterically, just in time!

This passage says that God exults over us with loud singing, and the first thing I imagine is being bounced on the knee of a joyful, boisterous father delighting in his child. What song is God singing? What kind of music does he like? It would seem that he loves to listen to music as well: the Bible is full of songs of triumph, love, praise and lament – whole books of them.

Praising God with music is not just a human whim. The heavens sing too, from the song of the angels at Jesus' birth to their songs of praise in Revelation, while the morning stars sing together for joy at creation (Job 38:7).

Ancient traditions of Christianity have imagined God singing, rather than speaking, the whole of creation into being, and creation itself is musical. Psalm 98 describes an orchestra of praise: the sea roars, the rivers clap their hands, the hills sing. Elsewhere trees and valleys clap their hands, and creatures of the deep sing along. God the musician conducts a cosmic choir and a symphony orchestra made for constant music. Every one of his creations is an instrument of praise, and each one is ready to take over when another falls silent. Jesus told the Pharisees that if the disciples stopped singing his praises, the rocks would strike up with their own tune (Luke 19:39-40).

One of my children hates the Happy Birthday song, but we're allowed to sing it provided that she conducts it. She loves doing that because she gets to be in charge: we speed up and slow down according to her beat; we stop when she brings us off and start up again when she raises her arms. We perform the song entirely to her timing.

God the musician conducts the orchestra of his creation with perfect timing. It's laid out in Ecclesiastes 3:1-8. 'For everything there is a season, and a time for every matter under heaven,' the famous passage begins, and what follows is like a song itself with its repeated rhythm: 'A time to be born, and a time to die… a time to weep, and a time to laugh… a time to keep silence, and a time to speak…'

Music is all about knowing when to keep silence. Nothing was ever more embarrassing in choir than coming in loudly on the soloist's verse, and it still smarts that I lost points in my grade seven cello exam for not having noticed two rests at the end of a well-rehearsed piece. Tuning is important, but timing and rhythm are everything, especially when more than one instrument is playing at once.

I don't think I've ever played in a musical group where the conductor hasn't reminded us at least once to 'Look up! Eyes off the music, please! Look at me!' If we don't watch the conductor, it all falls apart very quickly. God the musician, just like my daughter when we bring out a birthday cake, pulls the timing around: he brings in certain instruments and then others, he creates pauses and times of silence, he increases and decreases the volume, and the only way to join in is to look up and see what he's doing. When we do, we might even notice that he's singing along.

A suggestion

Do some loud singing today! It has physical benefits, lowers stress levels and can affect your emotions – and links your voice to the whole of creation in praise.

A prayer to God the musician

Great conductor of all creation, I add my song of praise to the rocks and trees, the valleys and rivers. Lift my face today so that I notice the rise and fall of your hands as they guide me into action, into silence, into quiet times or times of noisy celebration. Keep me in the rhythm of your music now and always.

10 December

Weaver

Psalm 139:13–15

For it was you who formed my inward parts;
    you knit me together in my mother's womb.
I praise you, for I am fearfully and wonderfully made.
    Wonderful are your works;
that I know very well.
    My frame was not hidden from you,
when I was being made in secret,
    intricately woven in the depths of the earth.

Come with me to an ancient Near Eastern house. It's probably made of mud brick, though the foundations might be laid in stone, and when we go inside we'll find a living area portioned out: a space for the animals and a space for the people. If there are two floors, the people will live above. There might be a little courtyard for the animals. Perhaps it isn't a house at all: if we've come across the home of a nomadic tribeswoman or a shepherd, it could be a tent. Whatever the living space is like, though, we'll find what we're looking for inside, tucked out of the way in a corner. Hanging from the ceiling (from a beam between two pillars, perhaps, or part of the structure of the tent) are long, thin strands of flax, linen or wool, each weighted at the bottom with a stone or clay weight. This is the loom. The long threads that hang vertically are called the warp. At the top, we can see the beginnings of the weft: the thread that is woven horizontally to and fro to make the fabric.

As we watch the inhabitants of the house going about their business, we'll notice that amid the chatting and cooking, the sweeping and washing, the coming and going of people and animals, a woman keeps coming back to the loom. Each time, she sends the shuttle back and forth, weaving another narrow thread horizontally between the warp thread, as many times as she can before the next interruption. She puts a pot of water on to boil; she waits at the loom. She puts the baby down to sleep; she sings lullabies from the loom. Her friend comes round to talk; she listens from the loom. Gradually, infinitesimally, the woven cloth grows, colours are added to the weft and patterns emerge. Meanwhile, to the children running in and out, the loom is a feature of the house, like wallpaper. They barely notice that day by day it grows and changes, until the finished fabric can be taken down and used for a blanket, a shawl, a shirt. Then the woman hangs a new, empty warp, and starts again. The whole family is clothed from her loom.

The image of God as a weaver in Psalm 139 is a very feminine one, which is perfect for the scene being described. The unborn child grows gradually, secretly, infinitesimally, in the woman's domain: the womb, the corner of the home, the loom. The word that has been translated here as 'knit' carries the meaning of fixing on and stretching out the warp threads, setting up the loom for a new piece of cloth; it's the very beginning of life, the work prepared and laid out, ready to start. The psalmist then praises the intricacy of the work, the complex patterns that emerge in the fabric of our own bodies.

Where God is described as a weaver in scripture, the cloth he is weaving tends to stand for a person's life and, specifically, for their allotted lifespan. So Job complains that his days are 'swifter than a weaver's shuttle' (Job 7:6); Hezekiah says, 'Like a weaver I have rolled up my life; he cuts me off from the loom; from day to night you bring me to an end' (Isaiah 38:12). This metaphor relies on the fact that the woman preparing her loom decides at the beginning how long the piece of fabric will be; she must make the warp threads a little longer than the intended length of the fabric. Once the warp is cut to fit the loom, one end on the beam and the other tied to a weight, it cannot be made longer. So in Psalm 139, straight after God's work as a weaver comes the image of all the psalmist's days being already written in God's book. The implication is that God already knows the length of a child's life and has a plan and a design for that child, even before he or she is born.

At first, this 'my days are numbered' edge to the metaphor makes God the weaver come across as rather sinister, sending the shuttle to and fro towards inevitable doom; but looking back at our weaving woman shows that the opposite is true. Each little bit of pattern, looking like nothing as she adds it thread by thread, grows through her design into a beautiful cloth. And when the cloth is removed from the loom, it's not the end of the fabric's life; it's the beginning. Now it can be shaped and worn and loved and shown off and used to wrap the baby in. Now it begins its useful purpose, the reason it was conceived in the first place. So the image of God the weaver used by Job and Hezekiah points them and us not towards destruction but towards completion by the God who intricately designs us and has all our days in mind from before our birth. This metaphor carries a hope of eternal life: we are intended, designed, for a life after death, a life away from the loom.

A suggestion

Find a quiet moment today to have a close, careful look at the weave or knit of a piece of your clothing. Use a magnifying glass, if you have one, and examine the intricacy and mathematics of it. See how far you can follow a single thread along. Then go back and read the verses from Psalm 139 again, praising God for making you so carefully and for continuing to weave new patterns in your life.

A prayer to God the weaver

Lord, thank you that you keep me always near you, your constant, careful work; I am safe in your house. The warp of my life is known to you; work with me in the weft, and, as you add to the unique pattern you have designed, help me to trust in your intention for my life.

11 December

Potter

Isaiah 64:8

> Yet, O Lord, you are our Father;
>   we are the clay, and you are our potter;
>   we are all the work of your hand.

2 Corinthians 4:5–7

> For we do not proclaim ourselves; we proclaim Jesus Christ
> as Lord and ourselves as your slaves for Jesus' sake. For it
> is the God who said, 'Let light shine out of darkness', who
> has shone in our hearts to give the light of the knowledge
> of the glory of God in the face of Jesus Christ. But we have
> this treasure in clay jars, so that it may be made clear that
> this extraordinary power belongs to God and does not come
> from us.

Taking part in a creative retreat, I wander along to the art room and ask for a bit of clay. I'm given one about the size of a walnut, and I sit down with it. The clay is firm in my hands, not pliable and elastic like the children's plasticine I'm used to. It is unwilling. It doesn't want to be rolled into a ball. Cracks appear on its surface. Eventually, I smooth it into a sort of cylinder, and I think I'll try to make a little pot.

I start to press a small dip into one end of the clay cylinder. More cracks appear. There is clay under my fingernails. It's all very gradual and slow, the dip becoming deeper. I get a bit impatient, but going too fast makes the clay protest, cracks appearing everywhere at once. Perhaps it needs some water?

There's something compelling about the image of God as a potter, which may explain its multiple appearances in scripture. Like the other images of God as a creative artist, it's a double metaphor: to say that God is a potter implies human beings are the clay, and that's specified by Isaiah. This metaphor carries more weight than the others, though, because isn't there some literal truth in it? Genesis 2:7 shows God modelling the first human out of clay, the dust of the earth. The image holds a deep truth about our mortality, our essence.

Now the clay is slimy, but the work is quicker. I press in and pull up the sides of my pot. A sort of vase neck is forming, not quite by design, where I'm grasping the pot. As the clay dries again (it dries quickly), long cracks start to appear around the neck of the pot and seem impossible to smooth over. The neck opens out into pieces like a flower. I start to smooth them to look more like petals, rounding the edges as if this was intentional. To get the last two even, I have to separate them, making a new break in the clay.

If God is the potter, then we are the clay; but within that image, more metaphors are layered. Are we the soft and malleable clay that, in Isaiah 64:8, would be foolish to deny the fingerprints and intention of its maker? Are we the spinning clay on the potter's wheel in Jeremiah 18, clay which seems to have a mind of its own, whose behaviour will affect its final form as the potter reshapes it? Once fired, are we brittle, fragile and disposable, or can we be useful for various purposes according to the potter's intention when he made us (Romans 9:20–24)?

Perhaps the best picture of humankind as clay comes when Paul extends the metaphor by adding treasure to the image of earthenware pots (2 Corinthians 4:7). Terracotta (literally, cooked earth) amphorae were the plastic bottles of ancient Rome: made for one use and designed to be disposable, but, unlike plastic, they came from the earth and returned safely to the earth. Put treasure inside one, and you have an image of a temporary, fragile body carrying something holy, eternal and so precious that it is easily worth risking the pot to transport and access the treasure.

We might imagine that other pots are more ornate, stronger or more valued than ourselves, but as Elihu points out to Job, we're all pinched from the same lump of clay – all made of the same earthy stuff. Paul says that it's the gospel, the treasure inside us, that deserves our attention and defines our purpose.

I hold up my pot-which-is-now-a-flower for a final inspection. Streaks of clay-filled water drip down to my elbows. I notice that every petal now has one of my fingerprints where I've pressed and shaped it – forensics could identify this clay as mine. It's not perfect, but it is pretty. I wouldn't want to squish it back into a ball; it's my creation. I've spent time with it. It wasn't quite what I was expecting to make, but here it is all the same. It's as if the clay helped, cracking where it did, to suggest the shape it now is. Bits of it are under my nails and caking my hands. We're connected, me and my little pot.

I carve my initials on the bottom.

A question

Which part of the pottery image most applies to your life at the moment? Do you feel that God the potter is slamming the air bubbles out of you before beginning his work, or are you being moulded and shaped? Are you being spun on a wheel, smoothed, glazed? Are you in the heat of a kiln? Talk to God the potter about what he is doing and how you are feeling about it.

A prayer to God the potter

Father, you are my creator. Your fingerprints are on me; the earthy mess of me is on your hands. You coax me, mould me, slam me down, guide me up. Repair me, Lord, reshape me when you find my flaws. In your patient loving kindness, keep making me as I am in your mind's eye.

12 December

Clothier

Matthew 6:28–30

'And why do you worry about clothing? Consider the lilies of the field, how they grow; they neither toil nor spin, yet I tell you, even Solomon in all his glory was not clothed like one of these. But if God so clothes the grass of the field, which is alive today and tomorrow is thrown into the oven, will he not much more clothe you – you of little faith?'

There's a field near my house that I love in every season, but in the height of summer it's breathtaking. The golden colour of the crop contrasts with the wide blue sky, and along the margin of the field by the footpath all kinds of wildflowers enjoy the tilled and fertile soil: red poppies standing out between buttercups, daisies and cowslips. I always think of Joyce Grenfell's comparison of the sight to a girl's straw hat trimmed with flowers.

Jesus wasn't standing beside a field in Suffolk, but his suggestion to 'consider the lilies' works for any flower. God's care and skill in clothing his creation is everywhere when we stop to gaze at it. His clothing of his people, however, has more to do with mercy than beauty.

God's first act of clothing humankind comes in Genesis 3:21, when he makes garments of skins for Adam and Eve. The clothing is a concession, a result of their shame, which is a result of their sin, but there's something very touching about God's not wanting them to leave the garden naked and ashamed. God's instinct, even in the middle of curses and consequences, blame and banishment, is to cover and ease his children's shame. As a metaphorical clothier, though, these basic coverings are not all God has to offer.

Unlike the disciples, I don't tend to worry about clothes, because I'm fortunate and have far too many of them. I seem to be in a constant cycle of trying to sort through them and give them away to charity shops, where I immediately buy more clothes. Standing in front of my wardrobe looking for the next things to weed out, I'm bewildered: I see woolies and T-shirts, boots and sandals, cocktail dresses for those events I never actually attend, my performance storytelling outfits in a range of bright colours, a pair of waterproof trousers I wore once in the snow, and my old college scarf, which, despite the moth holes, I can't quite bring myself to throw away.

Clothing protects us against weather and injury; it equips us for sport and work. So does God's clothing: 'Put on the armour of light… put on the Lord Jesus Christ,' writes Paul (Romans 13:12–14), not to mention the 'whole armour of God' listed in Ephesians 6.

Clothing identifies, too. My college scarf showed where I belonged in an environment where you could spot the students by their plumage. My bright storytelling colours and rainbow hat show that I am supposed to be waving my arms around and singing this way; I'm not just a rather strange member of the crowd! God's clothing identifies us as his. Paul writes:

> As many of you as were baptised into Christ have clothed yourselves with Christ. There is no longer Jew or Greek, there is no longer slave or free, there is no longer male and female, for all of you are one in Christ Jesus.
> GALATIANS 3:27–28

There's a Middle Eastern folk tale about a 'wise fool' who is invited to dinner with the king. He arrives in his work clothes, and the guards turn him away. Returning in dinner dress, he is welcomed in to the feast, but when the food is served he picks up the soup and pours it into his robe, saying that it was clearly his clothes that were invited to dinner and not him! It's a clever moral tale about our temptation to judge others by their looks and clothing.

Jesus, too, tells a story about a guest being kicked out of a feast for not wearing the right clothes (Matthew 22:1–14), but his parable is not about people judging each other by their looks; it's about whether we are wearing the clothing God has provided. When Jesus pointed to the lilies, he was talking about real, earthly clothing just as he had been talking about real, earthly food a few moments before, but there is always a deeper meaning when the Bread of Life talks about bread. In a world obsessed with identity and status, badges and slogans, a world of worrying about what we wear, God offers us spiritual clothes that make us equal to each other, make us one with each other and make us heirs with Christ.

A suggestion

Whenever you put a piece of clothing on today – a coat, shoes, a dressing gown – think about why you have chosen it and what you are wearing it for. Then ask yourself what kind of spiritual clothing you might need to put on at the same time, and take a moment to ask God the clothier to give it to you.

A prayer to God the clothier

Father, you know my frailty and my shame, yet you allow me to cover myself up. Even though I was not the one to toil or spin, I can come to your table clothed in Christ, your Son. May your clothing for me cover over my identities and snobberies, and all the ways I define myself by comparison with others, and instead allow others to see something of you in all your glory. Amen

13 December

Architect

Job 38:4–7

'Where were you when I laid the foundation of the earth?
     Tell me, if you have understanding.
Who determined its measurements – surely you know!
     Or who stretched the line upon it?
On what were its bases sunk,
     or who laid its cornerstone
when the morning stars sang together
     and all the heavenly beings shouted for joy?'

The creator God, speaking to Job, describes his work as an architect and a builder. Not only did he lay the foundations of this building himself, but he also carefully worked out its measurements beforehand and checked them, making sure that the plans matched the finished article. Here is God on his hands and knees, with the plans of the earth in one hand and the end of a measuring line in the other, marking out the foundations and laying the cornerstone of his design.

I don't know much about architecture, but a quick visit to Wikipedia suggests that the cornerstone is the first stone laid in the foundation of a building and that the other stones will be set in reference to its exact position and angle. In other words, the architect can't just plonk it down anywhere. The plans for the placement of the whole building need to measure up exactly to the cornerstone.

Laying the cornerstone of a building has always been a ceremonial moment. For an architect, it's the culmination of long hours spent poring over sketches and calculations, puzzling out where every stone will be placed and how the building will achieve its purpose. Now the dream becomes reality, the theories are put into practice and the stone from which every other stone in the building will be measured is placed. Throughout history, the moment has often been marked by acts such as prayers, offerings, the placing of a time capsule, the engraving of the architect's name, a dedication, a crowd of onlookers, a party. Likewise, in this image of God the architect, the morning stars look on and celebrate the occasion.

God the architect does not retire once the world has been built. In the New Testament, both Peter (1 Peter 2:5–8) and Paul (Romans 9:33) use the metaphor again, but this time God builds with living stones. The architect's carefully laid-out plans are for a building made of people. Both Paul and Peter refer to Isaiah 28:16, both pointing out that Christ is the cornerstone that God says he is 'laying in Zion' for this new building. At Christmas we see Christ the cornerstone being laid in a manger, accompanied again by joyful, heavenly singing.

What exactly is God the architect building this time? Paul explains: 'You also are built together spiritually into a dwelling-place for God' (Ephesians 2:22).

God is building himself a house.

If you're like me, you may need to stop and shake several catchy Sunday school action songs out of your head in order to hear the enormity of that statement. God, the architect and builder of the universe, who cannot be contained by any human structure, is building a living dwelling for himself out of human beings.

Solomon's temple, in 2 Chronicles 3—7, provides the root of this metaphor. Solomon builds God's dwelling with very precise measurements, and when it is finished, God enters it in glory. Paul and Peter must have had this temple in mind when they wrote about the careful building of a human temple where God will show up in power.

Solomon's temple replaced the tent that had housed the ark of the covenant ever since its journey through the wilderness. Throughout scripture, tents stand for transience, journeying and looking forward to a promised land; in 2 Corinthians 5:1, the tent is a metaphor for our earthly bodies, while God's building is the promise of an eternal home.

In the image of God the architect, therefore, there's a promise of eternal permanence. God is not only building an eternal home for us; he is also building an eternal home for himself, out of us. His work is not yet complete, but the cornerstone has been laid and the plans are all there, showing the precise placement of each stone, with each exact measurement sketched out. Just as he did at the creation of the world, God the architect gets involved, stretching his measuring line and checking the ongoing work until it is completed in eternity.

A suggestion

When you next look at the bricks and stones that make up your home or your church, think of the planning that went into the design. Where do you think you might be in God's plans for his dwelling? Can you imagine which room you would be a part of or where you would fit in with the other living stones around you?

A prayer to God the architect

Lord, in your plans there is a place for me. You have measured me exactly and you have worked out where I fit. Count me among your living stones and make your dwelling with me. Set me in reference to Christ the cornerstone, so that together with all the saints, I may grow into a holy temple by your Spirit.

14 December
Metalworker

Deuteronomy 4:15–20

> Since you saw no form when the Lord spoke to you at Horeb
> out of the fire, take care and watch yourselves closely, so that
> you do not act corruptly by making an idol for yourselves, in
> the form of any figure – the likeness of male or female, the
> likeness of any animal that is on the earth, the likeness of
> any winged bird that flies in the air, the likeness of anything
> that creeps on the ground, the likeness of any fish that is
> in the water under the earth. And when you look up to the
> heavens and see the sun, the moon, and the stars, all the
> host of heaven, do not be led astray and bow down to them
> and serve them, things that the Lord your God has allotted
> to all the peoples everywhere under heaven. But the Lord
> has taken you and brought you out of the iron-smelter, out
> of Egypt, to become a people of his very own possession, as
> you are now.

In the Genesis account of creation, it says that God created
humankind in his image. One of the ways in which we reflect God's
image is in our own creativity. All of these creator metaphors for God,
these different types of art and artist that describe God in various
ways, began as little nuggets of God's creativity in the human mind
and soul. It's no wonder that we can see God in them when they are
gifts of God in the first place.

Sadly, one of the themes of scripture is that people tend to take that
divine creative spark, that image of the creator God in us, and use it
to create God again in our own image. In Isaiah 41:7, there is a vivid

description of the crafting of idols with all sorts of technical words to explain how the metalworkers go about their business: smoothing with a hammer, striking an anvil, soldering, strengthening with nails.

When God compares himself to a metalworker, it's very often in the context of idol worship. Our passage today about being brought out of the iron furnace comes directly after a stern warning against idolatry. God seems to be pointing out the irony: 'I am the one making you, hammering, striking and shaping you, not the other way round.'

Israel's time of slavery in Egypt is compared to the iron furnace. Heat in metalwork has two purposes, and both are used in the various metaphors of God as the metalworker. First, the furnace softens the metal and makes it malleable so that it can be hammered into shape. In this case, Egypt is compared to the furnace, and Israel has been brought out of it, but perhaps their 40 years in the wilderness is the hammering and shaping of the softened metal into a useful form.

The second use of a furnace is to refine metal, and this image is used frequently throughout the Old and New Testaments, from Malachi 3:2–3, in which God sits in judgement as both the refiner's fire and the refiner himself, to Revelation 3:18, in which Jesus offers gold 'refined by fire' to the church in Laodicea. The refining fire melts away the metal alloys until pure silver or gold is left, while the dross of other, less precious metals is skimmed off and discarded.

There is a lot of loss in that metaphor. If God is refining us with fire, we may find that things we thought were a precious part of us turn out to be dross. God as refiner is melting away things that we are literally attached to, things that we felt belonged to us – because they had control of us. In the same way that the Israelites in the wilderness missed the security of their slavery in Egypt, we can sometimes hang on tight to sin and resist change.

There's another reason for this image to come up so often next to idolatry in the Old Testament: in just the same way that gold and silver are always ready to form alloys with other metals, people are always attaching themselves to idols. It's a human sickness. We look for things to follow, things beyond ourselves to rely on and blame and make into little gods. When we feel that we rely on something, that we really need it, it's especially difficult to let it go. When we have made something into a god, and we've made it in our image, sometimes we need God's help to let it go.

The end of the refining process is silver or gold, but getting there can be painful. Can we trust God the metalworker to discern what is gold and what is dross, when all of it seems so much a part of us? Can we allow ourselves to be softened by difficult experiences so that we are easier to shape? Do we believe that God will bring us out of the furnace and see, reflected in our new shiny surface, his own image?

Suggestion

Whenever you see your reflection today – in mirrors, shop windows, shiny spoons – use it as a reminder to think about how you are reflecting God's image to those around you.

A prayer to God the metalworker

Lord, sometimes I feel as if I'm in a furnace, being hammered and struck more than I can stand. I'm terrified of losing pieces of myself. Help me to rely on your vision for me: help me to trust that you are making me into the best version of me that I can be. Refine me and polish me until I reflect your image, Lord, my maker and redeemer.

At the end of week 2

- Which image of artist and artwork do you think best describes your walk with God?

- Which metaphor was the most surprising description of God? Why do you think that is?

- Are you an artist or creator of something? Perhaps you're familiar with one of the arts named in this chapter, or perhaps it's something not mentioned: cookery, painting, knitting, performance? How could those arts also become metaphors for God, and what do you learn about God through doing them?

- What could help you to remember that you are a beautiful work of art, being made and perfected by God the artist?

Week 3

GOD THE OWNER

There is a collection of parables told by Jesus in which God appears as a master, king or landowner. This week, we will have a look at this group of stories about how God runs his metaphorical household, kingdom or property.

That God has built something, and that he now owns it, is not too much of a surprise; we know that God has created the world, and it is his. The interesting thing about these parables is who God chooses to hold the reins of his property, what tends to happen as a result and how God reacts. In particular, we will focus on the emotions of the owner or master in each of the stories and consider how they fit with our idea of God. Even though God's emotions don't work in the same volatile way that human emotions do, these stories are as close as we can get to understanding God's response to our broken world.

This set of parables often seems to focus on a broken relationship or an essential misunderstanding about who the master of the household is. In many cases, the story centres around a servant who has made a wrong assumption about the character of their master. It's a good opportunity to check whether our assumptions about the character of God are correct or whether we might have made a similar mistake, especially when we think we know how God would react or what he would say.

Parables are not moral stories, pointing us to the way the world ought to be or the way we ought to behave; instead, they are true stories, describing to us the way the world really is and the way that we do behave. With that in mind, let's allow ourselves to be challenged and informed by these metaphors of God the owner.

15 December

Gardener: the God who waits and hopes

Luke 13:6–9

> Then he told this parable: 'A man had a fig tree planted in his vineyard; and he came looking for fruit on it and found none. So he said to the gardener, "See here! For three years I have come looking for fruit on this fig tree, and still I find none. Cut it down! Why should it be wasting the soil?" He replied, "Sir, let it alone for one more year, until I dig round it and put manure on it. If it bears fruit next year, well and good; but if not, you can cut it down."'

I know nothing about gardening. Our garden has always been a meadow. I pretend I'm leaving it that way for the wildlife, but really it's just that I've had neither the time nor the knowledge to sort it out. The only thing I know about gardens is how to enjoy sitting in them. Sometimes I dream of being able to pay a full-time gardener to landscape and plant our garden from scratch, then lovingly keep it growing and flowering and looking beautiful, so that I could wander about in it like one of Jane Austen's characters. I'd have a table by a pond where I could sit and write, a labyrinth in which to walk and ponder the next chapter, a place for herbs and vegetables, roses growing over a trellis and a garden swing. Of course, this fantasy would in reality entail moving house as well as employing a whole team of gardeners!

In Jesus' parable about the fig tree, God is represented as two different kinds of garden-lover at once. He is the owner of the garden:

the one who walks in it, enjoys it and benefits from its produce. He has the final say in its design and what it contains. At the same time, in this parable, he is also the keeper of the garden: the one who gets his hands dirty, who digs and plants and prunes, who knows the way to take care of everything in the garden.

These two roles are reflected in God's character from the beginning to the end of the gospel story. God the garden owner strolls in his garden in the cool of the day, looking for Adam and Eve, who should have been looking after it for him, but who have already disobeyed, taking fruit from the tree that was not theirs to touch. At the other end of the story, a second Adam rises from the grave and walks through the garden, where Mary Magdalene takes him to be the gardener, the keeper of the garden – which is exactly who he is.

In the parable, there is once again a tree, which should be producing fruit – its figs are for the garden owner, and he has been waiting for them. For three years, the garden keeper has been working around this tree, but it has remained fruitless. It's taking precious nutrients from the rest of the soil. The garden owner wants to do the sensible thing and cut it down, but the garden keeper asks for one more year, another chance for the tree to respond to the seasons. He will give it special treatment, digging around it and fertilising it. After that, he says, if the tree is still fruitless, the owner of the garden can cut it down.

Three years was the length of Jesus' ministry on earth, and I wonder whether he told this parable with some frustration or exhaustion in his voice as he looked at the results of his work so far. But the parable holds the frustration in balance with the hope of the garden keeper that the tree can still bear fruit. As a parable, it holds a warning – that time is running out to repent and listen to Jesus' teaching about the kingdom. As a story, though, it holds an image: God the garden owner, a God of justice, with God the garden keeper, a God of mercy, standing together by a fruitless tree. The image holds justice and mercy in tension, so that we could almost imagine this as a repeating scenario: the owner always wanting to cut the tree down; the gardener always pleading for one more year; the tree always deserving destruction and receiving mercy. God the gardener is waiting, peering at the buds and leaves, digging around the roots, endlessly hoping that we will bear the fruit of faith and repentance and return to him in the garden.

A suggestion

Look outside today and see if you can find anything growing. Tricky in December! As you look at the empty winter trees, ask yourself whether there is an area of your life that is feeling empty and fruitless. What kind of fruit would you like to be able to offer to God the gardener in the spring – perhaps an area of your work, a character trait you'd love to show, a talent you feel you could be using more? Ask God to dig around your roots, and wait with him.

A prayer to God the gardener

Dear Lord, some of my branches have been fruitless for a long time. There are talents and skills I'd love to grow and develop and use to your glory. And the fruit of your Spirit – love, joy, peace, patience, kindness, goodness, faithfulness, gentleness and self-control – there are plenty of times when I could use all of those! Thank you for keeping me safe in your garden. Please do some digging around me, some nurturing and some pruning, and with your help, Lord, may I grow those fruits.

16 December

Rich master:
the God who invests

Matthew 25:14–30

> 'For it is as if a man, going on a journey, summoned his slaves and entrusted his property to them; to one he gave five talents, to another two, to another one, to each according to his ability. Then he went away. The one who had received the five talents went off at once and traded with them, and made five more talents. In the same way, the one who had the two talents made two more talents. But the one who had received the one talent went off and dug a hole in the ground and hid his master's money.'

vv. 14–18

I couldn't believe it when I saw the name on the flyer. I had to run to my bookshelf to make sure I'd recognised it correctly. I found the slim, yellow book I was looking for and read the signature in the front. Sure enough, this was the poet who, nearly 20 years ago, read my poems when they were mostly teenage drivel and didn't seem put off – in fact, he made notes on each of them and met up with me and my cello teacher in a little cafe in Sevenoaks to go through them one by one. I hadn't seen him or heard of him since. Now he was giving a workshop in our neighbouring town. I had to be there.

After the workshop, I approached the poet and explained that 20 years ago, my cello teacher had passed him a folder of my poetry while they sat together in a London orchestra.

'Did I respond?' he asked.

When I gratefully told him that he'd done much, much more than merely respond, but had actually annotated the dreadful poetry with sincere and helpful advice and then met up with me and gone through every poem, he replied, 'Oh, I'm so glad I did; because someone did the same for me, before my voice was really formed. A poet I respected read my poetry before it deserved to be seen, and I've always been grateful for her generosity.'

He went on to praise the poetry I had produced in the workshop, evidently delighted that I was still writing and that my own voice had developed. His investment of time and expertise in me as a young poet, which had made all the difference to my work and life, had in turn come from a similar investment made in him.

In this parable, the master has invested his property – huge sums of money – in his servants. It's not just the money that he expects to grow; it's the servants themselves, as his trust in them should encourage them to take responsibility and develop their own skills. The master has given each servant the means to go far.

When the master returns and receives his money again, his joy and relief are evident, not in receiving the money but in praising the servants. He rejoices that they have met his expectations, and he welcomes them to share in his joy: they're not just being sent off penniless now that their job is done, but they are being invited to share in the celebration and to take on more of the household, continuing their relationship of trust with their master. He invested in them, and now he enjoys their success with them.

The servant who buried his single talent in the ground is lacking that relationship, because his understanding of the master's character is all wrong. Instead of seeing the coin as an investment, he saw it as a burden: a heavy responsibility and work that was pointless, because the master would 'reap where [he] did not sow' and take the money away again. The one-talent servant could see the money, but he couldn't see the investment that the master was making in him, in his own abilities.

That's the danger in losing sight of the fact that everything we have to work with comes from God: we start to think we've gained it all ourselves, and then we wonder why we owe any of it back. None of the servants could have produced anything without the master's initial investment.

If we think of God as a hard taskmaster, expecting us to work until we drop and then being unhappy with what we produce, we will end up burying his investment in us and feeling bitter. But God in this parable is much more like the poet who annotated pages of bad poetry for a teenage girl. He invests generously in us despite our shortcomings, and he has high expectations that one day he will return and look at our work and be delighted with what we have managed to do with his gifts.

One phrase the poet used stuck in my thoughts: 'She read my poetry before it deserved to be seen.' It resonates with a familiar phrase from the Communion service: 'When we were still far off, you met us in your Son…' God has invested in us far more than mere money, time and talents. His investment was his own Son, so that through him, we could not possibly fail.

A question

When has someone invested in you? How could you use and celebrate that investment today?

A prayer to God the rich master

Thank you, my master, for investing in me. It's amazing to me that you not only value me, but want to equip me to grow and develop, to use my little talents in your great kingdom. Keep me in mind of how much you have spent on me. I love to think of us celebrating together.

17 December

Landowner:
the God who grieves

Matthew 21:33–40

> 'Listen to another parable. There was a landowner who
> planted a vineyard, put a fence around it, dug a wine press in
> it, and built a watch-tower. Then he leased it to tenants and
> went to another country. When the harvest time had come,
> he sent his slaves to the tenants to collect his produce. But
> the tenants seized his slaves and beat one, killed another,
> and stoned another. Again he sent other slaves, more than
> the first; and they treated them in the same way. Finally he
> sent his son to them, saying, "They will respect my son." But
> when the tenants saw the son, they said to themselves, "This
> is the heir; come, let us kill him and get his inheritance." So
> they seized him, threw him out of the vineyard, and killed
> him. Now when the owner of the vineyard comes, what will
> he do to those tenants?'

When my husband was exploring his vocation to be ordained in the
Church of England, a diocesan vocations advisor came to interview
me, his fiancée, as a prospective vicar's wife. It was less an interview
and more a checklist of warnings. Did I realise that we would be
moving house fairly often, especially at first? Did I understand that
my house would be a workplace as well as a home, with people
coming and going all the time? Was I prepared to start a family in a
clergy house instead of choosing where we lived?

Living in a clergy house certainly has come with blessings, frustrations and a number of interesting moments, but mostly it's the weighty sense of responsibility that I wish I'd been warned about. We don't own our house, but we don't rent it either: it's tied accommodation that comes from the diocese and has to be returned to them in a reasonable state at the end of our stay. I moved into our current house with a two-year-old and a four-month-old baby, and there have been times when I've sat on the stairs scrubbing pen off the wall and wondering how much the diocese is going to hate us when they get the house back. (I have heard rumours that some areas have a Diocesan Book of Shame, with photos of messed-up vicarages that get sent ahead to your next parish. I really, really hope the rumours are not true.)

This parable is all about bad tenants, and the tenants of the vineyard are like those of a clergy house in that they have been placed there as stewards, not as renters or buyers. They are there to look after the place rather than to gain or take from it. They are there to continue the work of the owner, and the vineyard and the fruit still belong to him.

The details at the beginning of this parable outline the owner's special care for the vineyard and his pride in it. He has done everything for its success and poured love, money and sweat into the project. The vineyard has everything it needs to produce a good crop; all it will take is some people to look after it while the owner is away.

The problems start when the owner of the vineyard sends servants to collect the harvest. The tenants react by beating the servants and sending them away empty-handed or even killing them. It is unclear whether the tenants have produced fruit and kept it for themselves or simply let the vineyard go to waste so that there is no fruit. What we can see clearly is the position of the owner.

The vineyard owner in the story shows us a God who created something and loved it; he let someone else use it and it was smashed up, stolen, ruined. There is personal hurt, grief and confusion. Why would they treat him and his beloved vineyard like this? The work and expense have all been his, and yet the tenants seem to think that they have some claim to the fruit of the vineyard. When the master's own son arrives, they are somehow deluded enough to imagine that by killing him, they will be able to keep the vineyard, the son's inheritance. They clearly don't imagine a scenario in which the master might come back himself to claim his property, let alone think about what he might do to those tenants in his anger and his grief. Perhaps they think that the master doesn't care about the vineyard or that he will never come back. Perhaps, in their self-satisfied triumph, they have forgotten that he exists at all.

The parable was a warning to the Pharisees, but it asks some helpful questions of us, too. What if everything and every person around us belongs to God? What if we are here to look after his kingdom? What are the fruits that we owe him? Do we ever manage to persuade ourselves that our lives are our own, that we can make the rules? And if we push away the people who try to tell us that isn't so, and if we kill the Son who comes to us with our words and actions, do we remember that there is a God who grieves over his children and his ruined creation?

A question

During Advent, Christians look forward to the time when Jesus will come again to take charge of our broken world and rule in peace. Do we really believe and live as if he will?

A prayer to God the landowner

We are sorry, Lord. We forget too easily that these precious things and people we have around us are gifts. Too often our words hurt others, and our greed and selfishness destroy the good things you have given us. Too often we push even your Son away and block our ears, wanting to imagine for a little bit longer that we can be in charge. We are sorry, grieving God. We hand it all back to you. Come in, and make your kingdom happen in us, on earth as it is in heaven.

18 December

Merciful king: the God who is passionate about mercy

Matthew 18:23–35

> 'Then his lord summoned him and said to him, "You wicked slave! I forgave you all that debt because you pleaded with me. Should you not have had mercy on your fellow-slave, as I had mercy on you?" And in anger his lord handed him over to be tortured until he should pay his entire debt. So my heavenly Father will also do to every one of you, if you do not forgive your brother or sister from your heart.'
>
> vv. 32–35

What are the issues that really get you in the gut, the ones that can make you cry when you see the news? These days, with charities able to advertise on social media, and dozens of news outlets able to stream video to our phones, we can experience compassion fatigue – a self-protective numbing to the sights and sounds of distress. Even so, we often find that there is one issue, perhaps just one image, that breaks through our barriers and twists our hearts, making us angry, emotional and determined to act. It will be a different issue for everyone, based perhaps on our own past experiences or whether it has affected someone we love. It will move us deeply every time we come across it. It will keep us awake at night.

For me, it is anything to do with children in trouble, and most recently it was images of refugees in camps on Lesbos that caused such a reaction. Children who had made terrifying journeys across the sea in leaky rafts, who had seen members of their family drowned, were now gathered outdoors in knee-deep mud with nowhere to go. They were burning plastic bags to try to keep warm, breathing in the toxic fumes as they huddled around in freezing, damp clothes. Sending money didn't stop my feeling of desperation for them. I longed to leave my own children in our warm, cosy home, and fly to Greece with warm sleepsuits and coats. I prayed constantly for the rain to stop in Greece, because it was all I could do. I checked the charity's website repeatedly for news of whether my prayers were working. I was taken over by it for weeks.

The king in this parable is an example of someone who is motivated by an issue just like that. For him, it's forgiveness and mercy, or rather the lack of them, that cause that gut reaction and inform the way he acts. Not only does the king compassionately agree to forgive an enormous debt, but when he sees even a small mercy refused he flies into a rage and seeks immediate justice.

The king does try, briefly, to play by the rules. At the beginning of the story, he makes arrangements for his slave and the slave's family to be sold, which is a logical reparation, in those days, for so much money having been lost. He knows that the slave will never be able to repay his debt. But the moment he actually sees the slave pleading with him, his compassionate response is sparked, and he offers mercy. He can't help it. Face-to-face with distress, and in a position where his forgiveness can solve the problem at once, he acts.

When the slave immediately fails to forgive a smaller debt owed to him, Jesus mentions that his fellow slaves 'were greatly distressed'. The whole household, belonging to their master, shares his sense of justice and recognises the need for mercy; it distresses and moves them just as much as it does him. This tiny piece of information shows us something more about the character of the forgiven slave, in that he has somehow been impervious to this shared knowledge, this important household value. Somehow, even now that he has experienced its outworkings directly, this slave has managed to stay in his own bubble, to remain selfishly absorbed with what is owed to him.

It's that attitude that now enrages the master. Doesn't this slave see, hasn't he only just seen for himself, that forgiveness and mercy are the most important things? How has he not understood how vital forgiveness is as a value in this house? The same fierce compassion that had mercy on the slave now exacts justice, because it's the value of forgiveness itself, rather than the future of the slave, that motivates the king.

In this parable, we see a God who is motivated by the issue of forgiveness. It's what brings tears to his eyes when he sees it on the news or when it comes up on his social media feed: every angry word and bitter exchange, every retaliation. He longs for his household to live in peace with him and with each other.

Of course, God is not a human being like the master in the parable, so it's not quite that the issue of mercy moves him and drives him to act. He doesn't need that reminder: his values and emotions are constant. It's more that God *is* mercy and will always be that way.

It's why he forgave the world; it's what sent him to die on the cross; it's the purpose behind his final words of mercy to the soldiers that nailed him there, to the thief that hung beside him. Through Jesus, it's his attitude towards us, all of the time, even though we could never possibly pay him what we owe.

A question

If it causes distress to the master, then it causes distress to the rest of his household. Is there a small or a big thing that you could do today, as part of God's household, to bring about forgiveness and mercy, to mend a relationship or put a grievance to rest?

A prayer to God the merciful king

Lord, thank you for your compassion. Thank you for your mercy towards me, your endless forgiveness for me. Please show me where I still need to forgive, small debts and large, and please help me when it's so hard to let go of the hurt. Make me a member of your household, distressed by the things that distress you, echoing the longing of your heart for peace.

19 December

Employer:
the God who is despised

Matthew 20:1–16

> 'Now when the first came, they thought they would receive
> more; but each of them also received the usual daily wage.
> And when they received it, they grumbled against the
> landowner, saying, "These last worked only one hour, and
> you have made them equal to us who have borne the burden
> of the day and the scorching heat." But he replied to one of
> them, "Friend, I am doing you no wrong; did you not agree
> with me for the usual daily wage? Take what belongs to you
> and go; I choose to give to this last the same as I give to you.
> Am I not allowed to do what I choose with what belongs to
> me? Or are you envious because I am generous?"'

vv. 10–15

In every generation, there have been little pieces of advice handed
down from parents to children, and through many generations they
have stayed the same. Don't talk to strangers; say no to drugs; don't
drink when you're thirsty (that one comes from my dad, and he was
referring to alcohol); always wear clean underwear and carry five
pounds (my mother-in-law, who first said it in the days when five
pounds could buy you a taxi ride home).

These days, parents have a new maxim for 21st-century teens: 'Never
read the bottom half of the internet.' The comments sections can
turn ugly very quickly and seem to be full of people drunk on their
relative anonymity, out to make trouble and cause arguments.

Strangely, comments left under good news stories are very often the ugliest. If somebody has helped a homeless person or raised a huge amount of money for charity, or if a sick child has been visited in hospital by their favourite celebrity, don't read the bottom half of the internet. It will be full of people complaining: people shouldn't help the homeless! No, they should help *all* homeless people, not just one while being filmed! They raised the money to get attention! They chose the wrong charity! That celebrity shouldn't have disturbed that poor child's family!

One line in today's parable struck me, in verse 15: 'Are you envious because I am generous?' A note in the NRSV says that the original Greek is literally translated: 'Is your eye evil because I am good?'

Why do people react to goodness with evil and complaint? What makes us quicker to judge and find fault with good news than with bad? Perhaps it's because we have been challenged, made to feel that someone is better than we are. Or perhaps it's a symptom of something much darker and deeper in the human condition.

The workers who complain in the parable are feeling hard done by, despite the fact that they have been paid a fair day's wages, exactly as they agreed. There wouldn't be a problem if the employer had not chosen to pay the same amount to people who came long after them and did a fraction of the work. It's always in comparison to others that we start to feel overlooked and complain that life isn't fair. At first glance, the workers seem to have a point, but we can see their mistake when we notice, as the employer points out, that they're not asking for more for themselves – they are asking for someone else to have less so that they can feel better. 'I choose to give to this last the same as I give to you,' says the employer. 'Is your eye evil because I am good?'

The evil eye is a way of cursing somebody. The employer feels cursed: despised because of his generosity, rejected because of his goodness. His good deed has been turned on its head in the eyes of the world so that it comes across as evil. For Christians today in the public sphere or even just on social media, it's a recognisable situation and one that can bring huge anguish. It happened to God first, and still happens every day, that people see his goodness as evil, interpret his justice as inequality and reject his perfection as less valuable than the world's brokenness.

Within a parable about God's fairness to others, there is a hidden parable about our unfairness to God. Despising goodness is the ultimate injustice, but how often have I envied someone else's success or felt grouchy because a friend seems especially blessed while things are going worse for me? Is my eye evil because God is good?

A suggestion

Go on to social media, find a good news story and say something kind about it. If you're not on social media, try to spot a good or generous deed today and say something encouraging to the person who did it, or call a friend to congratulate them on their success.

A prayer to God the employer

Lord, the whole universe belongs to you, and you choose blessing. You choose to pour even yourself out for us. You have blessed me with [name what you can think of here] and I thank and praise you. When I see your blessings for others, may I remember all you have given me, and rejoice with them.

20 December

Host: the God who is disappointed

Luke 14:16–24

> Then Jesus said to him, 'Someone gave a great dinner and
> invited many. At the time for the dinner he sent his slave to
> say to those who had been invited, "Come; for everything is
> ready now." But they all alike began to make excuses. The
> first said to him, "I have bought a piece of land, and I must
> go out and see it; please accept my apologies." Another said,
> "I have bought five yoke of oxen, and I am going to try them
> out; please accept my apologies." Another said, "I have just
> been married, and therefore I cannot come." So the slave
> returned and reported this to his master. Then the owner
> of the house became angry and said to his slave, "Go out at
> once into the streets and lanes of the town and bring in the
> poor, the crippled, the blind, and the lame." And the slave
> said, "Sir, what you ordered has been done, and there is still
> room." Then the master said to the slave, "Go out into the
> roads and lanes, and compel people to come in, so that my
> house may be filled. For I tell you, none of those who were
> invited will taste my dinner."'

My husband and I had our first marital argument about three hours
into married life, during the wedding reception. It was about the
place cards. We had gone to the venue ahead of our guests, with a
box of table centrepieces and the place cards to lay out according
to our meticulously well-thought-out plan. His job was to bring
the diagram we'd made of where all the guests would sit, but he'd
forgotten it.

I couldn't believe it! The waste! The hours we'd spent figuring out where all these people would eat their dinner! Nestled in each centrepiece was a photograph of a different church to which one or both of us had a connection. We'd planned it as a conversation starter, so that at least one person on every table would recognise the church and know the connection. We'd worked out who to sit with whom so that nobody would feel left out or less welcome. It had taken ages.

Eventually, I stopped lamenting and panicking, and we shuffled through the place cards and worked it out all over again, and, of course, it was easy. Looking at the names of our guests and picturing them in the places they were about to sit and celebrate with us was a joy. Each guest was so special to us, and we were excited to see them.

So it is with the feast in this parable. Every guest is named, wanted, planned for. But all of them have something better to do, and they don't seem to understand the thought and love that have gone into their place at the table. It matters that they are not there, but they have no idea. Perhaps they think that their absence won't even be noticed.

When nobody turns up, the host understandably reacts in anger and frustration. There are places ready, set out with expensive food and drink. If the invited guests aren't going to eat and drink it, then somebody else jolly well is! And the host's first thought is for the ones who will really appreciate the banquet: the poor, the crippled, the blind and the lame, the beggars sitting in the streets of the town or taking the lowest-paid jobs in the field. From this reaction, it's clear that the host's purpose in throwing the banquet was never to show off or to rise in social circles; it was all part of an honest celebration and because he likes to see guests sit and enjoy their food. Perhaps the original guests suspected strings attached, but they were wrong. The host loves to provide a good feast, no matter who eats it.

There are really two metaphors for God in this parable, because while he is the host, he is also the feast. It's himself he invites us to take part in. He loves to watch us finding enjoyment and life, and to see us being strengthened, when we feast on him. There is always some vulnerability in inviting new acquaintances for a meal or a party, hoping they'll like what we have to offer and, by extension, us. Here is that vulnerability increased and exemplified by a God who offers himself as the feast and the purpose of the gathering.

The parable finishes with the host encouraging the servant to fill every place at the table, because 'I tell you, none of those who were invited will taste my dinner'. I wonder what tone of voice Jesus used to tell that part. Is the host saying, 'Fill up every chair, so that if any of those previous guests later changes their mind, they won't get a look in'? Or is it a disappointed acknowledgement: 'They are really not going to show up, so come on, let's make sure every place is filled'? Knowing the generosity of God, I lean towards the latter.

In context, the parable carries a basic message to the leaders Jesus is addressing: if the people of Israel reject their Messiah after this long time of preparation, then their places will be taken by the Gentiles. More broadly, it holds a general message: God continues filling his heavenly feast until it's full, and he does so not with the people we might expect – not necessarily with the rich or religious or important but with outcasts, the ones who never thought they'd get in. But beyond its straightforward meanings, the parable shows us a picture of God and the value he places on each individual invitee. Imagining the disappointment, sadness and frustration crossing the face of God the host as he realises that his beloved friends won't be there after all makes me want to send my RSVP straight away.

A question

Everyone you meet today has an invitation to be a valued guest at God's banquet. How will that affect the way you see them?

A prayer to God the host

Dear God, thank you for your invitation to the feast. Thank you for pouring yourself out for me. I can't wait to be there at your table, sharing your banquet.

21 December

Woman who found it: the God who rejoices

Luke 15:8–10

'Or what woman having ten silver coins, if she loses one of them, does not light a lamp, sweep the house, and search carefully until she finds it? When she has found it, she calls together her friends and neighbours, saying, "Rejoice with me, for I have found the coin that I had lost." Just so, I tell you, there is joy in the presence of the angels of God over one sinner who repents.'

A few summers ago, on a sandy beach by a lake, I took off my rings so that I could apply sun cream. I slipped my wedding ring and engagement ring together into a pocket of my handbag and forgot all about them. It was only that evening, after getting back to my parents' house, that I went looking for them and discovered they were gone. I knew at once what must have happened: the open bag had tipped up, and the rings must have slid out into the sand.

I was distraught, but I was ready to give the rings up for lost. The lake and beach were closed now. Even if we went back the next day, surely we had no chance of finding two tiny pieces of white gold buried in the sand on a beach full of people?

It was my father who talked me into it. Armed with a colander, we arrived at the lake before it opened and begged our way in. Using a flag by the water as a rough marker of where we had been sitting, we began to dig and sift, shaking sand through the colander while watching for a glint of sun on metal and listening for a telltale clink. Nothing. Soon the lakeside opened, and curious people came over, asked what we were doing and then laughed and walked away. Impossible!

We had been there a good hour, and made a deep hole and a tall pile of sifted sand, when my father called my name and held up the engagement ring. I couldn't believe my eyes. He really had found it! With renewed enthusiasm, we went back to sifting the sand where he had discovered it. The sun was beating down now and we were sweltering, having not thought to bring water or sun cream with us, but we couldn't give up now; since we had the engagement ring, we knew for sure that the wedding ring was there somewhere.

My dad went off to buy some water, and it was just as he was coming back that I stood up and screamed, 'I've found it!' All the earlier mockers were suddenly around us, their laughter no longer scornful, congratulating us and exclaiming in wonder. I had both rings back on my finger! We went home to celebrate with wine and cake, and of course I did the 21st-century equivalent of inviting all my friends to the party – I posted it on Facebook.

In all the other parables in this chapter, God has been represented as the owner of some large property, land or household, even as a king in charge of a country. But everybody has responsibility for something, however big or small, and in this parable Jesus uses the example of a woman who owns ten coins. Each coin is a drachma, about a day's pay on minimum wage; the woman is not very rich, and each coin is more important to her in her poverty than it might have been to some of Jesus' listeners.

To find the coin, the woman lights a lamp, which is an expense in itself as it will burn oil. She sweeps the house, looking out for that glint of lamplight on silver, listening for the chink and scrape of metal across the floor. How many hours does she search? How many times does she go around that house, wondering if there's a dark corner she's missed, a piece of furniture she hasn't moved? The task seems impossible. The only thing that keeps her looking is that she knows it's there. She knows she lost it in the house, so she will surely find it there if she just keeps looking.

God keeps looking for us because he knows that we're there. He made us and we are his, and he knows that we are retrievable; however lost we are, however many years it's been, however impossible it may seem that we would love him again, he will keep searching because he knows that there is a way for us to be found.

When the woman finds the coin, it's so wonderful, so amazing and so unlikely that she has to tell everyone. She rushes out rejoicing and calls her friends and neighbours to marvel and rejoice with her.

This parable offers a beautiful antithesis to the others that we've read in this section. We have seen God disappointed, hurt, angry and grieving over the loss of his property, but here we see God rejoicing, relieved and delighted as the last little bit of his precious possession is restored to him. So he is, says Jesus, when one person turns back to him; and so he will be when at last the whole world is restored.

A suggestion

Take a moment to bring to mind all your most precious things: anything that would be devastating if you lost it, perhaps something that you did lose and still wish you could find. You are that precious, and so much more important, to God.

A prayer to God the finder

God, searching with your lamp: may I search with you? Let me light a lamp and sweep as well. Send me into dark corners; let's sift through this dust together. I'll trust and hope with you that this whole world can be restored again. When we find your precious treasure, let me rejoice with you.

At the end of week 3

- Which of these parables were familiar, and which had a new emphasis for you?

- Does the owner in each of the parables sound like the same character, or do they all sound like different people? In what way?

- Which owner or master did you feel the most sympathy for? And which servant or tenant did you sympathise with the most?

- Many of these parables are read or referred to during Advent, as they are pictures of a world waiting for the return of its owner and master. What do you think it looks like to be ready for Christ's return?

Week 4

VEILED IN FLESH

As we draw closer to Christmas Day, it's time to look again at those familiar characters in the nativity story: the holy family in the stable, the shepherds in the fields, the strange visitors journeying to find the newborn king.

We could look into the stable and see not just the unfolding of the Christmas story but also a collection of scriptural metaphors for God. In the Bible, God is described as a father and as a mother, as a shepherd and as a king, even as a midwife.

This week we will look at the ways in which God is compared to each of the nativity characters, pausing, of course, on Christmas Day to see God appearing on earth as a tiny human baby in a manger. It's the moment we've been waiting for.

22 December

Bridegroom

Isaiah 62:3–5

> You shall be a crown of beauty in the hand of the Lord,
>   and a royal diadem in the hand of your God.
> You shall no more be termed Forsaken,
>   and your land shall no more be termed Desolate;
> but you shall be called My Delight Is in Her,
>   and your land Married;
> for the Lord delights in you,
>   and your land shall be married.
> For as a young man marries a young woman,
>   so shall your builder marry you,
> and as the bridegroom rejoices over the bride,
>   so shall your God rejoice over you.

As a vicar, my husband has seen his share of brides who are late to their own wedding, but none has been more nerve-racking for him than the very first occasion. He was a newly ordained deacon, and only there to observe, but it very nearly ended up with him having to officiate the wedding! The barriers at a level crossing had become stuck down, with the groom and the church on one side – and the bride and her father, in their car, on the other. The vicar, who had another service to get to, launched into a crash course in filling in the wedding registers. After half an hour of worried glances at the clock, passers-by lifted the barriers manually to allow the bride to arrive, and the ceremony got underway just in time to stop the new curate being thrown in at the deep end!

Plenty of brides are 'fashionably' late, to the frustration of their vicars. One priest in Kent appeared in the national papers after he imposed a £100 fine on brides who were over ten minutes late, though he said he had never yet had anyone late enough to pay it. Joseph, however, may have been kept waiting longer than any bridegroom in history. Somehow, he managed to wait patiently through discovering that his fiancée was pregnant, making plans to end their relationship, being called off by an angel, processing the news that the baby was going to be the Son of God, being called away by the census to Bethlehem and watching his newly homeless wife give birth outside an inn.

Yet Joseph's part in the familiar nativity story is a little picture of a big metaphor used by God to describe his relationship with his people. However long any earthly bridegroom has been kept waiting, God has been infinitely more patient. Throughout the Old Testament, Israel is often referred to as a faithless woman, constantly straying out of relationship with the God who loves her. The prophet Hosea even underwent a literal marriage to the adulterous Gomer as a picture of God's faithful love repairing this broken relationship. But in this beautiful passage from Isaiah, God the bridegroom is looking forward with longing to the time when he will finally be able to take Jerusalem as his wife. Lovingly, he imagines the wedding: she will be a crown of beauty, a royal diadem. Never again forsaken or desolate, she will change her name to reflect her new status, and he will delight in her and rejoice with her.

It's the same vision that John sees in Revelation 21:2: 'the holy city, the new Jerusalem, coming down out of heaven... prepared as a bride adorned for her husband'. Anyone who has attended a wedding is familiar with the moment depicted in that image, the moment when the music plays and the bride first enters the church.

In May 2018, Prince Harry married Meghan Markle, and as she entered St George's chapel in Windsor castle, every eye and camera turned to look at her radiant face, her beautiful, simple gown and her long veil. There were cheers from outside the church. She began to make her way up the aisle as the cameras zoomed in on her face. But then they turned to look at the prince, moved to tears by the sight of his approaching bride. 'You look amazing,' he whispered as she reached him.

That's the moment God the bridegroom is waiting for: he will rejoice over his bride when she comes to him at last. As we spend Advent waiting, not just for Christmas but for the day when Jesus comes again to claim us as his bride, we can know that God the bridegroom is waiting with us, and for us, with just as much longing, excitement and love.

A question

As part of the church, which is God's bride, what could you do today to show your love for the bridegroom?

A prayer to God the bridegroom

Lord, sometimes the waiting feels so heavy and so long. Sometimes I begin to doubt that there will ever be an end to this waiting and hoping and longing. It helps to know that you are waiting, hoping and longing too, a bridegroom looking forward to his wedding day. What a wonderful moment that will be, when you first set eyes on your church and she on you. Keep us patient and busy in the waiting, Lord, our bridegroom.

23 December

Father

Luke 15:11–32

'"I will get up and go to my father, and I will say to him,
'Father, I have sinned against heaven and before you; I am
no longer worthy to be called your son; treat me like one of
your hired hands.'" So he set off and went to his father. But
while he was still far off, his father saw him and was filled
with compassion; he ran and put his arms around him and
kissed him. Then the son said to him, "Father, I have sinned
against heaven and before you; I am no longer worthy to be
called your son." But the father said to his slaves, "Quickly,
bring out a robe – the best one – and put it on him; put a ring
on his finger and sandals on his feet. And get the fatted calf
and kill it, and let us eat and celebrate; for this son of mine
was dead and is alive again; he was lost and is found!" And
they began to celebrate.'

vv. 18–24

Jesus taught his disciples to see God as a good father. To their
surprise, he told them to pray to 'Our Father in heaven', and they
heard him using the familiar term 'Abba' to describe this Father who
was so much better than earthly fathers. I wonder whether Joseph
was ever in Jesus' mind when he used the image of a father to explain
God to his disciples. The man who had adopted him, cared for him,
protected him and taught him must have been a great model for an
earthly father, even if he did not always fully understand his son's
extraordinary purpose or his close relationship with his heavenly
Father.

But in this story that Jesus told, we have an image of a God who is a bad father – at least, he is by any earthly standards. He's the father who can't control his children, the father who gives his boys whatever unreasonable thing they want rather than exercising discipline or saying 'No'. He's a father who has somehow ended up with one son who wants him dead, so that he can have his inheritance already, and another who seems to think that his dad is a kind of slave driver, unfeeling and unjust; one son who can't get away fast enough, another who only stays out of obligation and feels bitter about it.

This is a father who lets his son go and gives him up for dead: a father who sits at home staring out of the window while his other son, the obedient one, does all the work without being asked, and feels more and more hard done by as time goes on.

It's a father who sees his son returning, filthy and destitute, having spent every penny of a lifetime's earnings he didn't work for, and, instead of flying off the handle or locking all the doors, races out barefoot in his underwear halfway through shaving, in full sight of the neighbours, to embrace his child. The boy isn't even particularly remorseful, only hungry and out of other options, but he gets clean clothes and a huge feast and the fatted calf that was reserved, like a vintage wine, for some far more important occasion: the older brother's wedding, perhaps.

And when the older brother finally finds a voice and objects, he just gets told to come along to the party, because, after all, nobody told him to do all that work and he never asked for so much as a goat. If he had, he might have discovered that his dad would do anything for him, too.

He's a tragic father, really. Nothing is too good for either of his beloved boys; it's just that neither of them ever bothered to get to know him and find that out.

What if there had been a third son in the story, one in between the two extremes? A son who neither ran away nor saw his father as a tyrant to be obeyed, but who lived happily with him, shared in what they owned as a family, worked out of love and followed his father's heart in agreement with him?

Perhaps that extra son would have tried to persuade his younger brother not to leave. Perhaps he would have sat with his father by the window, hoping every day to see his brother come home. Perhaps he would have come alongside the older brother and showed him a way of working that didn't feel like drudgery, and encouraged him to ask their dad for something and see what happened. At the end of the story, the extra son would have joined the celebrations without question, because his values are his father's values and, anyway, how could he resist rejoicing when he saw the joy on the father's face?

If Jesus had put that son into the story, he would have been talking about himself, which is why Christians believe that it's through Jesus that we can be children, too, adopted into the same perfect relationship with our heavenly Father. A reading from *The Cloud of Unknowing*, which we had at our wedding, translated, says: 'Love is so powerful that it makes all things shared in common: therefore love Jesus, and everything that he has will be yours' (ch. 4). Jesus is the perfect Son, and everything that he has is his inheritance: his divine family, his heavenly home, his eternal life. Loving him makes those things our inheritance, too, and makes his Father our father.

God our Father is loving because is love. He can't help it. He's compassionate because we belong to him and he is connected to us through and through. He longs to have us home again, and he longs for us to know that everything he has can be ours.

A suggestion

Read the parable again, in a version you love, and see if you can imagine yourself there. Which of the brothers has your sympathy? If you were in that house, how would you relate to the father?

A prayer to God the father

Our Father, whose home is heaven,
your name is holy!
May your kingdom arrive here, and your will be done here,
*   until earth looks just like heaven.*
Give us everything that you know we need, because everything
*   you have is ours if we ask.*
Forgive us the things we do wrong: forgive us the times we run
*   from your instructions, and forgive us the times we resent*
*   them.*
Help us to forgive our brothers and sisters, just as you have,
*   even if they have hurt us. May we join in their welcome*
*   parties.*
Don't let us be tempted away from your house. Deliver us
*   from evil.*
We love you, Father.
Amen

24 December

Midwife

Romans 8:22–23, 26

> We know that the whole creation has been groaning in labour pains until now; and not only the creation, but we ourselves, who have the first fruits of the Spirit, groan inwardly while we wait for adoption, the redemption of our bodies... Likewise the Spirit helps us in our weakness; for we do not know how to pray as we ought, but that very Spirit intercedes with sighs too deep for words.

It's Christmas Eve. Our little Mary and Joseph figures have finished making their long journey around the house and reached the stable, where they have settled down. After church tonight, I shall quietly place the tiny baby in the manger with them, to the wonder of the children when they find him there in the morning.

If only it had been that easy for the real Mary and Joseph. I wonder what Mary was doing at this point before the birth of Jesus? When did her labour start? Was she – horrible thought! – labouring for hours or even days while she travelled?

I wonder whether Mary had a midwife. The word literally means 'with woman', and there are only a very few cultures in the world in which a woman has ever been expected to give birth alone. Midwifery has existed since prehistory for advice, support and the crucial moment of catching the baby. The various stages, signs and potential problems that can occur during labour would have been shared knowledge among women, in the days before general education and professional medicine. Mary would have been expecting to have at least her mother and any sisters around her – perhaps even her cousin Elizabeth, the one who would most recently have been through the same experience. Instead she found herself alone. Perhaps Joseph raced up into the inn and asked some of the local women for help.

In the Psalms, God is referred to as being present at births like a midwife: 'Yet it was you who took me from the womb; you kept me safe on my mother's breast' (Psalm 22:9), picturing the moment when the midwife first catches the baby and lifts it straight away into its mother's arms to start nursing.

God the midwife appears at more cosmic moments, too. In Job 38:8–9, God is pictured catching and swaddling up the sea in clouds and darkness after its birth, a strangely tender image in a verse about the strength needed to contain the sea. A midwife's care for the baby straight after birth is invaluable as the mother begins to recover, and in a culture where infant death was commonplace and infanticide was not unknown, midwives would have saved hundreds of lives. (The midwives present at Moses' birth, Shiphrah and Puah, did save his life and were important enough to be named in the narrative.) God the midwife swaddling the sea is an image of preventing disaster, controlling a situation as dangerous, unpredictable and messy as a birth.

But the real value of the midwife is not just at the birth itself, but during the long labour before it. Some of these midwife moments have been lost in modern medicine or replaced by the woman's partner or a doula, but a midwife should be there for most of the last part of labour, the part when it gets hard. A midwife supports and comforts the woman as the contractions grow more intense and come closer together; a midwife tough-talks the woman at the moment of transition, when she wants to give up altogether. The midwife knows that transition, the moment when the pain is worst and the body is taking over control, means that the baby is about to be born, and her knowledge carries the mother through. The midwife may remind the mother to breathe, may pant and breathe along with her to regulate her breathing.

In today's reading, God is the midwife for the whole of creation in labour. Paul writes that we, as well as all creation, are 'groaning together in the pains of childbirth' (Romans 8:22, ESV), waiting to be set free, waiting for the new creation. In the image, we are both the mother in labour and the child waiting to be born, because we are groaning 'while we wait for adoption, the redemption of our bodies' (v. 23). But, in verse 26, the Spirit is there, groaning alongside us. God the midwife, who understands the timing of the birth from the hardest moments of the labour, shows creation how to groan, how to wait, and reminds us that, as Paul says earlier in verse 18, 'the sufferings of this present time are not worth comparing with the glory about to be revealed to us'.

As Mary looked down at her new baby, the memory of the previous hours and days dropped away. Glory had been revealed in a brand-new, tiny face.

A suggestion

Today, whenever you see evidence of the groaning of creation – in the news, in people around you, in your own suffering and waiting – take a moment to lean on God the midwife. Regulate your breathing, and focus on it. Imagine God breathing and groaning with you. Think of the glory soon to be revealed.

A prayer to God the midwife

Lord, the state of the world can fill us with despair. From those closest to us, to tragedies taking place in far countries, the pains of creation are everywhere and they overwhelm us. Lord, groan with us while we groan, breathe with us and show us the rhythm of your breathing. Bring to birth in us your new kingdom, your new creation.

25 December

Baby

Luke 2:7

And she gave birth to her firstborn son and wrapped him in bands of cloth, and laid him in a manger, because there was no place for them in the inn.

This book is full of metaphors for God: ways in which God has been 'carried across' to the world. Some, like the burning bush or pillar of cloud, were chosen by God himself; other beautiful images from the Psalms were inspired by God and written by poets, always trying to come closer to understanding every facet of our awesome God. But the very fact of reading all these metaphors shows us how huge, how ungraspable, God is. We can only see a little bit of him at once, and even those glimpses are imperfect comparisons, fleeting images.

Today is Christmas Day. Emmanuel, 'God with us', has arrived. God as a baby is not just a metaphor, or, rather, he is the most literal of all metaphors, because rather than being a simple comparison, in this baby God really has been carried across to the world. He is what we've been waiting for. He is the image of the invisible God.

Today will be a busy day for many people; for others, perhaps, it will be a quiet or a sad one. Christmas means that God is with us, wherever we are, whatever we're doing and whoever we're with. Rather than a long reading, I would like to offer you a poem to contemplate, in however much time you have today. Come and gaze at this longed-for baby.

Incarnation

How perfect for God to call us this way:
the irresistible invitation of being small,
the invitation of the infant, mute, wide-eyed,
the rooting mouth's silent innate call,
and the turning of his head to the side,
the clasping clench of the tiny fist,
which, given no more than a fingertip,
refuses to let go.

A suggestion

However you celebrate today, find a moment to worship at the manger.

A prayer to God the Christ child

Lord Jesus, you are so small, so vulnerable as you come into
our world.
May I see you as Mary did: with eyes full of love, longing to lock
eyes with you for the first time.
May I see you as Joseph did: with relief and wonder at the
delivered promise of your birth.
May I see you as the angels did: with songs of praise echoing
back and forth through history.
May I see you as the shepherds did: born for me, born for the
poor, the ordinary, the searching, the humble.
May I see you as the magi did: a new king, a high priest,
a sacrifice.
May I see you with my eyes, too, and in my heart, this Christmas
and always.

26 December

Mother

Isaiah 49:13–15

Sing for joy, O heavens, and exult, O earth;
    break forth, O mountains, into singing!
For the Lord has comforted his people,
    and will have compassion on his suffering ones.
But Zion said, 'The Lord has forsaken me,
    my Lord has forgotten me.'
Can a woman forget her nursing-child,
    or show no compassion for the child of her womb?
Even these may forget,
    yet I will not forget you.

'So, what has motherhood taught you about God?' My visiting friend smiled over at me as I nursed my newborn daughter. I looked down at my baby's tiny face, considering the question. She was only a few weeks old, but we had already had our share of troubles: in her first week of life she hadn't been feeding properly, resulting in a traumatic hospital stay from which we were both still recovering.

'So far, motherhood has taught me how much God hates sin,' I replied. My friend, who had presumably expected me to say something fluffy about love, looked rather shocked. I tried to explain the direction my thoughts had taken.

'I just can't stand anything going wrong for her,' I said. 'Even little things like hunger or being a bit too cold, let alone the needles and treatments that she needed. She is too little to understand or expect or manage any of it, and I just have to watch her not coping with it.

I would change the whole world for her not to have to go through a single moment of pain. And I'm sure that's how God feels about sin and what it does to us. He just wants to wipe it out. I mean, I think I'm understanding the story of the flood for the first time.'

My friend nodded warily, and probably made a mental note not to ask that question to any more tired mothers of newborns!

Now, with nearly a decade having passed since that day, I'm much more sanguine about seeing my children go through the knocks and challenges of everyday life; but I don't think I want to change my answer. I have simply never experienced anything like the fierce compassion – in the most literal sense of the word, 'suffering with' – that I had for my new babies. That feeling is exactly what is meant by this passage from Isaiah: God is even less likely to forget Zion than a nursing mother is to forget her child.

In other words, it is impossible for God the mother to forget, turn away or refuse help when the children are suffering. Being a nursing mother is very physically as well as emotionally intense. If a mother ever did, in an exhausted moment, forget to feed her baby, even if the baby didn't cry, her body would soon remind her of the baby's need! Every nursing mother knows that if you are away from your baby, even if you've left your child in good hands and prepared plenty of bottles for the babysitter, your body will still remember the feeding times and start to produce the milk. God the mother is even more deeply connected to us.

That is a difficult truth to read for anybody who is suffering or crying out to God. There are times when we feel neglected or ignored by God, when our prayers seem to go unheard and dreadful tragedies happen in our lives and the lives of those we love. Just like the people of Zion, we feel forgotten and forsaken.

But God the mother has not forgotten. Just as I sat in the hospital while doctors tried to put a cannula in my baby's arm, tears streaming down my face in the knowledge that there was no way my week-old daughter could understand why such a horrific thing was happening or why I wasn't stopping it, so God the mother hears our distress and somehow sits with us through it, however forsaken we feel.

I would have done anything to take my baby's place and go through the pain for her. With the same compassion, God found the way, ultimately, to do that for us. Jesus' arrival as a baby was the beginning of God not just reaching out to show us that he was with us, but suffering what we suffer and dying to destroy the death that would have been ours.

A question

How do you react to the idea that God cannot forget you?

A prayer to God the mother

When I am hurting, you cradle me in your arms, my Mother. Your compassion for me is fierce and protective. You are my place of safety, of nourishment and of calm: though you cannot help me to understand the pain, still comfort me through it, God. Still keep me here in your arms.

27 December

Shepherd

Ezekiel 34:15–16

I myself will be the shepherd of my sheep, and I will make them lie down, says the Lord God. I will seek the lost, and I will bring back the strayed, and I will bind up the injured, and I will strengthen the weak, but the fat and the strong I will destroy. I will feed them with justice.

Every year in the Pyrenees, shepherds leave their homes in the valley and lead their flocks up to the mountains about 50 km away in a sort of pastoral pilgrimage known as transhumance. Whole communities of shepherds move together and stay with their flocks from July to September in small huts in the mountains. Every morning, they lead the sheep from where they have slept around the huts up to the richest pastures 1,000 metres high. The shepherds' job is also to milk the sheep, and in the same little mountain cabin they produce the result: my favourite cheese!

Ezekiel 34 is a lengthy extended metaphor in which God is the owner of a flock of sheep. He has left hired shepherds in charge of his flock, but they have been slack in their duties, making the most of all the perks of being a shepherd (constant roast lamb and woolly jumpers) but doing none of the hard work (fighting off wild animals and providing pasture and water). The chapter is a letter from the owner of the flock. He is on his way to sort things out, to replace the useless hired hands and to do some proper shepherding.

God's actions as a shepherd are shown up in the contrast between him and the hired hands. He gathers them, journeys with them, feeds them, heals them, judges between them and protects them.

First, God the shepherd gathers. He goes looking for the sheep who have wandered off. He's been gone so long that they are all over the place, but he brings them back, one by one if necessary, into the fold. They will come from different peoples and different countries, but God the shepherd knows where to find them.

God the shepherd journeys with his sheep. He leads them into the mountains where the good pasture is, and he knows when the time of year has come to leave the mountains behind. Unlike the hired shepherds, God doesn't abandon the sheep or let them find their own way; wherever they go, he travels with them.

In the pastures, he makes sure that they are fed, rested and strengthened, and he binds up the ones that have been injured on the journey. At this point, he also pays close attention to the sheep. Which ones are suspiciously fat? Which ones have been pushing their way to the front, stirring up the mud with their feet and hogging the drinking water by wading around in it? 'I will feed them with justice,' says God the shepherd. Enough for everybody, and any sheep that eats more than its fill should be careful. Being the fattest and biggest is a dangerous position for a sheep.

Finally, God the shepherd promises to protect the sheep from the wild animals that threaten to steal and destroy them. All the sheep in his care can trust him for peace and safety. This shepherd will stay awake while the sheep are sleeping, and risk his life, if necessary, to fight off wolves and bears.

It's no wonder that, in John 10, when Jesus called himself the good shepherd and made exactly the same promises, people picked up stones and said he was blaspheming. His listeners knew just what he was referring to, and they were frightened. The hired hands were in the presence of the owner of the sheep.

A question

What do you most need from God the shepherd at the moment? Do you need feeding, binding up, guiding to better pasture, protection from wild animals or from other sheep? How can you bring that need to your shepherd today?

A prayer to God the shepherd

With you as my shepherd, Lord, what could I possibly need? You lead me to the richest pasture and the freshest water; you bind me up when I am broken; you stay with me to protect me against every danger. You feed me with justice, keeping your eye on the bigger sheep. With you as my shepherd, I will follow you wherever I go. I know that I can trust you.

28 December

King

Zechariah 9:9–10

Rejoice greatly, O daughter Zion!
    Shout aloud, O daughter Jerusalem!
Lo, your king comes to you;
    triumphant and victorious is he,
humble and riding on a donkey,
    on a colt, the foal of a donkey.
He will cut off the chariot from Ephraim
    and the warhorse from Jerusalem;
and the battle-bow shall be cut off,
    and he shall command peace to the nations;
his dominion shall be from sea to sea,
    and from the River to the ends of the earth.

On 16 November 1940, the mayor of Coventry, John Moseley, was only just getting up and dressed when there was a knock at the door. He groaned, blearily making his way down the stairs. He had only been mayor for five days, but he had been awake for most of the previous 48 hours since the devastating blitz on Coventry on 14 November. He had spent long hours inspecting the terrible bombsites and helping with support and emergency planning. The mayor's wife, Nell, was still picking pieces of glass out of the carpet where their own windows had blown in, and she shouted out to whoever was at the door that they would have to go round the back, as the front door had also been damaged and was jammed shut. John made his way to the back of the house to see who their visitor was – and couldn't believe his eyes. 'Heavens above, it's the king!' he shouted. 'We'd better look sharp!'

King George VI made many tours of the blitzed cities, always dressed in his military uniform (he had served in the British fleet in World War I) and intent on raising morale. He had not announced this visit publicly, and rumour has it that he even brought his own packed lunch, knowing how precious resources would be on the ground with hundreds of newly homeless people. Mayor John Moseley, still unshaven but feeling much more awake suddenly, led His Majesty around the worst-hit areas, and King George famously stood in the ruined shell of Coventry Cathedral. His unexpected visit made a huge difference, bringing hope and comfort to the citizens of Coventry (and, presumably, went down in Moseley family history as 'the time John nearly met the king in his pyjamas').

These verses from Zechariah show two contrasting aspects of God as king. They describe a triumphant entry, perhaps a return from battle: a victorious king, a king who has saved and who is righteous and true, rides towards his people, who shout and sing to welcome him. Then, in the same breath, the prophet says that the king is 'humble and riding on a donkey' (v. 9). The verse comes after eight verses of destruction and judgement on all of Israel's enemies, but after this appearance of the king on the donkey, the mood changes: God the king may have been fighting, but his arrival heralds a rule of peace, a time with no need for chariots or warhorses. That's what the donkey in this prophecy signifies: the war has already been won, so there is no need for the king to appear in military force. An age of peace and safety is beginning.

The prophecy, like most prophecies, looks forward to more than one point in time. It speaks of the defeat of Israel's enemies at that time. It also heralds a day that we hope for even now, when the whole world will be peaceful under the reign of God the king. And it points to a familiar moment in between, a moment when Jesus rode into Jerusalem on a donkey. He wasn't returning from a battle, but about to go into one: a battle he would eventually win against death and sin. The people who waved palms didn't know or understand that. They were expecting a military hero to overthrow the Roman rule, but Jesus rode a donkey and reminded them of the much bigger picture: a prophecy about a God whose reign would be eternally peaceful, a king who has no need for a warhorse or a chariot, the Prince of Peace.

In some ways, Jesus' appearance in the world is rather like George VI's in Coventry. Although the war is still raging, although we suffer and fight, here comes the king unexpectedly: on foot through the vegetable patch because the front door isn't working, right into the middle of our everyday lives. He comes dressed as someone who has fought alongside us, who knows our battles. He doesn't mind that we haven't shaved or that we can't offer him a meal. He's brought his own sandwiches; he'll even share them. He's here to help. He'll know what to do. The war goes on, but when the king stands in the ruins of our lives, we know that we can have hope.

A suggestion

Show God the king around your life as you move through today: both the ruined parts and the parts that are still standing. Imagine him with you, taking an interest and offering his support.

A prayer to God the king

Your Majesty, you are sovereign, the Lord and ruler over my life, but you don't rule from a distance. Instead, here you come, picking your way through the rubble towards me. You inspect the mess that the latest onslaught has left, then you are ready with your plan of action. Lead on, my king. Let me follow you to the end of the world, until everything is peaceful under your eternal reign.

At the end of week 4

- Where would you place yourself in the Christmas story, or in the nativity scene?

- In some traditions that light the candles on the Advent wreath for nativity characters, the shepherds are linked to joy, and Mary to love. What abstract noun do you think best fits each of the characters you have read about this week? Are they words you readily associate with God?

Week 5 until Epiphany

VISIBLE IN CREATION

All the time, we are surrounded by tangible, practical, necessary things: things that we can experience directly with our five senses, things that we know intimately as part of our lives. It's these things that are so often used in scripture to draw our attention to some aspect of God. It may seem especially odd, even blasphemous, that a huge, incomprehensible God should be described as something tiny like a seed, inanimate like a rock or weak like a sapling, but these things that we know best can be the metaphors that carry God across to us most closely. In this extended final week (nine days to take us through every remaining day of Christmas until Epiphany), as we meet and worship God described in everyday parts of his own creation, may we remember that he is with us, all around us and within us, all the time.

29 December

Bread

John 6:32–35

> Then Jesus said to them, 'Very truly, I tell you, it was not Moses who gave you the bread from heaven, but it is my Father who gives you the true bread from heaven. For the bread of God is that which comes down from heaven and gives life to the world.' They said to him, 'Sir, give us this bread always.' Jesus said to them, 'I am the bread of life. Whoever comes to me will never be hungry, and whoever believes in me will never be thirsty.'

For health reasons a few years ago, I attempted to go gluten-, egg- and dairy-free for a while. It was bad enough that I could no longer make cakes without resorting to magic, but for a long time this meant going without bread. I missed it desperately. I picked disconsolately through the expensive gluten-free versions on the supermarket shelves, trying them all by turns: bread that fell apart when you buttered it, bread that had turned to crumbs in the packet by the time you got it home, bread that tasted as if it was still the potato flour it was made from and bread that was essentially sour cake.

Then our wonderful neighbours, who had a bread maker (several levels of domestication above my cookery skills) worked out how to bake gluten-free bread at home. Every now and then they brought it round, still warm, wrapped in a tea towel. I accepted it droolingly, and ate the first slice while the butter (well, all right, the dairy-free spread masquerading as butter) would still melt into it. So filling, so comforting, so good.

It's no wonder that, in the wilderness, the first thing the devil thought to offer Jesus was bread. After 40 days of fasting, I expect the sandstone rocks were already beginning to look like loaves even before Satan's cunning suggestion. Why not make them into the real thing? Wouldn't it be fitting for the Son of God to do? Isn't that exactly what God does in the wilderness – provide manna, the bread from heaven?

Jesus replied with a scripture: 'One does not live by bread alone, but by every word that comes from the mouth of God' (Matthew 4:4). That verse is given in Deuteronomy as the lesson that should have been learned by Israel from their experience of receiving manna during their 40 years in the wilderness: rely on God more than bread. 'He humbled you by letting you hunger, then by feeding you with manna… in order to make you understand that one does not live by bread alone' (Deuteronomy 8:3). The lesson of manna is to rely fully on God, to hunger for God's word in the same urgent, needful way that you hunger for bread, even recognising that without it you will die.

When Jesus says that he is the bread of life, he is not only talking about being the warm, filling, necessary staple that you crave. All of that is true, but he is also saying that he is a specific bread, the bread from heaven. He is referring to the manna in the wilderness.

Everybody listening would have known the story: how the manna appeared in the morning, covering the ground, and how they called it 'What's that?' because that's what they said when they came out of their tents and poked at it, and the name stuck; how it looked like coriander seed but tasted like honey; how it had to be shared equally, the same amount for each family, and anybody attempting to take extra for their own gain simply ended up with an inedible pile of maggoty manna; how there was never too much or too little of it, for 40 long years; and how it became the fragile difference between living and dying for a journeying people.

Jesus was making a very logical comparison in identifying himself as manna. After all, if we do not live by bread alone, but by every word that comes from God, and if Jesus is the Word of God made flesh, then it makes sense that he really is heavenly bread. Spiritually sustaining, necessary for life, he is equally available to everyone; but not in a way that can be exploited or hidden.

Bread has to be broken, sliced or crumbled to be shared. For Jesus to call himself the bread of life, he was also referring to himself as an offering, a sacrifice. Here is the bread that I need, at my door, wrapped in a white cloth. It is given for me. I can reach out and take it.

A question

The Israelites went out to gather their share of manna every morning. How could you gather your share of Jesus, the bread of heaven, to last you through the day?

A prayer to God the bread

Bread of Life, I am hungry for you, weak without you. You are broken for me, given to me. Feed me, sustain me, be always enough for me: teach me to share you, too, with those who hunger.

30 December

Water

Jeremiah 17:7-8

> Blessed are those who trust in the Lord,
>   whose trust is the Lord.
> They shall be like a tree planted by water,
>   sending out its roots by the stream.
> It shall not fear when heat comes,
>   and its leaves shall stay green;
> in the year of drought it is not anxious,
>   and it does not cease to bear fruit.

As I write, we have just had a summer of alarming drought and heat. Terrible forest fires raged across Europe while scientists continued their dire warnings of climate change. Closer to home, the newspapers were full of photographs of once-verdant parks and village greens, now just dust and brown, dead grass. Traces of ancient buildings began to show up on lawns, outlined where the foundations were a little deeper and the grass had stayed slightly greener than the scorched blades around it. Ponds dried up, and even the little stream that runs through our village was dry enough that you could walk along the cracked bottom. Fish congregated in a shallow puddle and had to be rescued. Our lawn turned yellow and didn't need mowing all summer.

We spent some time boating on the Norfolk Broads, and the change in the landscape was remarkable. It was still very hot, but from our boat we had a view of green fields and beautiful gardens, watered by the river. Trees growing on the banks looked healthy and strong. It was a picture of this passage in Jeremiah, and another in Psalm 1, comparing a person who trusts God to a tree planted next to the water. In this image, God is the river, a constant stream of water giving life to the tree. Someone who trusts in man, Jeremiah says, is more like a shrub in the desert – without God, away from the water, as dry as our scorched lawn and dead garden in the drought.

The part that stands out to me, though, is how the tree itself is feeling. It 'shall not fear' when heat comes, and 'in the year of drought it is not anxious'. When it should be at a crisis point, the tree is calm, knowing that it can rely on the water in the river.

Crisis points will always come. Trusting in God does not guarantee anybody a life of peace and plenty. The passage says 'when' heat comes, not 'if'. But God the living and constantly flowing water prepares us for the inevitable drought, the crisis times, the heat of stress and sorrow, the dark times and the doubting times, and we don't have to do anything beyond having our roots in the right place. Even in a year of drought, when terrible things keep happening to us and the ones we love and the world outside, and when God seems distant and silent, a deep river will keep watering us and our leaves will stay green.

Much later, in John 4, when Jesus meets a woman at Jacob's well and offers her water that would mean never being thirsty again, when he calls himself the water of life, he recalls that same picture of deep-rootedness and calm. He is calling the woman, and all of us, to be trees planted by a river, so that we don't need to worry about looking for water anywhere else. Other sources of spiritual comfort or refreshment will always run out, but God's river of living water never dries up.

So how do we make sure that our roots are planted in the right place? What does that look like in real life, when it comes out of the metaphor? In today's passage, Jeremiah says that it's about trust in the Lord. Putting our trust in God means that whatever happens, it's God that we turn to, God that we rely on, God where our hope lives.

It's difficult to have that kind of trusting faith. Sometimes I feel that I'm on the cusp of it; at other times, I see people who really do have that reliance on God, see how deep it goes in them and the kinds of trials it gets them through, and realise how much deeper my own roots still need to grow.

It's not easy, but every time we choose to trust God's promises instead of imagining that we can get through in our own strength, we creep a little closer to the river. Once we get there, we will not be anxious. There may be a year of drought and there will be heat, but there will always be deep, flowing water.

A suggestion

Think of one difficult or uncertain situation from your past or present, and try to imagine what trusting God in that place would look like and how it would feel.

A prayer to God the water

Water of Life, sometimes I fear the drought, the time of heat and trouble. I am anxious about the times when you seem further away. I watch others go through them, and I wonder how they manage, how their faith stays so green. Be a deep river for me when my soul is parched. Flow to the root of me and help me to stand tall when the heat comes, knowing that I do not need to fear.

31 December

Seed

John 12:23-24, 27-33

> Jesus answered them, 'The hour has come for the Son of Man to be glorified. Very truly, I tell you, unless a grain of wheat falls into the earth and dies, it remains just a single grain; but if it dies, it bears much fruit... Now my soul is troubled. And what should I say – "Father, save me from this hour"? No, it is for this reason that I have come to this hour. Father, glorify your name.' Then a voice came from heaven, 'I have glorified it, and I will glorify it again.' The crowd standing there heard it and said that it was thunder. Others said, 'An angel has spoken to him.' Jesus answered, 'This voice has come for your sake, not for mine. Now is the judgement of this world; now the ruler of this world will be driven out. And I, when I am lifted up from the earth, will draw all people to myself.' He said this to indicate the kind of death he was to die.

When did you last blow a dandelion clock? It may be a children's game, but I still find them irresistible. Did you know that a single dandelion head may have about 180 of those white, floaty seeds to blow off, and each one of those seeds can grow a new plant which will produce up to 2,000 more seeds altogether? This may explain the state of my garden.

Seeds, sowing and fruit were obviously powerful images to Jesus. In the parable of the sower in Matthew 13, the seeds represent the word of God falling on the different soils of people's hearts. Those who are ready with good, deep soil can receive the seed and produce fruit. Straight after that parable, Jesus tells another one about an enemy who sows weeds among the wheat of a farmer's field, so that the two have to grow together until the harvest. Immediately after that, Jesus uses a mustard seed to represent his kingdom, starting small and spreading into a huge tree that provides shelter.

Already, in all these parables, we can begin to see links between Jesus and the seed. Jesus explained to his disciples that the seed in the parable of the sower stood for 'the word of the kingdom' – but what does that mean? The message of the kingdom is inextricable from the message of Jesus himself and what he came to do – it is through him that we can receive the kingdom. When Jesus sent his disciples out to preach the good news of the kingdom, that good news was and is Jesus himself.

The word of the kingdom is a message going out from God to his people. Jesus, who is the Word of God, acts in the same way as the seed: he is sown on the earth to bring God's message and God's salvation to humanity. In the parable, the various places where the seed falls are like the hearts of people, hearts that are either ready to receive him or too hardened against him, too shallow or too full of other worries to have room.

Then, in our verse for today, Jesus uses the metaphor of the seed directly about himself and in almost exactly the same way that he refers to the seeds that grow at the end of the parable of the sower. Unless a grain of wheat dies, he says, it remains alone; but if it dies, it bears much fruit. The first three seeds in the parable of the sower remain alone, never having the chance to produce more grain. Only the final seed that falls on the good soil produces fruit.

So what does Jesus mean when he refers to himself as either remaining alone or producing fruit? The answer comes in verse 32: 'And I, when I am lifted up from the earth, will draw all people to myself.' The image is rich in meaning: the lifting up recalls the bronze snake that Moses lifted up in the wilderness, which healed all who looked at it from their snake bites (Numbers 21:9). The phrase 'lifted up' also looks forward to Jesus being lifted up on the cross, which, in a mirror image of Moses' snake, is our healing from the sin brought about by that original snake in Genesis. Beyond that, 'lifted up from the earth' also foretells the ascension: Jesus lifted up above the earth, glorified in heaven. But there's yet another image in it as well, because when a seed has grown into a full ear of wheat, it is lifted up from the earth in harvest. So we have a picture of Jesus the seed who was planted in the earth, grew up full of grain and will be lifted up – harvested, full of fruit; and the fruit that this God-seed has grown is all people.

In other words, when Jesus is lifted up and the harvest comes, all people will be lifted up and harvested along with him. This refers both to the cross, by which all people can be saved, and to the resurrection, in which all people will one day share when Christ returns.

Paul called Jesus 'the first fruits of those who have died' (1 Corinthians 15:20). The festival of the first fruits was celebrated at the beginning of the grain harvest, and until the first fruits of the grain had been offered as part of the celebrations, none of the rest of the grain could be harvested. In referring to Jesus as 'the first fruits', Paul is saying that Christ's resurrection from the dead is something that we can all expect. His death bore the first fruits, showing what the rest of the harvest would look like: our own harvest will follow his.

Just as, in the parable of the sower, a single planted seed grows to yield hundreds of grains, so the single buried seed of Jesus' death grows into a full ear of grain. We, the church, the body of Christ, are part of the fruit of Christ's body planted as a seed. In this image of a full ear of wheat, every individual grain is a person, drawn to Jesus by his death and his planting in the earth.

A suggestion

Have a look outside and see whether anything is growing yet. Gardens can look very dead at the end of the year, but we know that there is life hidden and beginning underneath. Consider what seeds in yourself you would like to see growing in the new year, and what fruit you would like them to bear.

A prayer to God the seed

At first you were tiny, no more than a word, an idea, planted in my mind, working your way into the soil of my heart. Put down roots in me, grow in me, until your fruit shows in me. May I plant you in others, because when you were planted in me I began to live.

1 January

Door

John 10:7–10

> So again Jesus said to them, 'Very truly, I tell you, I am the gate for the sheep. All who came before me are thieves and bandits; but the sheep did not listen to them. I am the gate. Whoever enters by me will be saved, and will come in and go out and find pasture. The thief comes only to steal and kill and destroy. I came that they may have life, and have it abundantly.'

Did you use an Advent calendar to lead up to Christmas this year? We generally end up with several in the house, given by kindly friends and relations: these days they offer not only chocolate, but also small collectable toys or parts of a building set. Last year I spotted one for adults containing 24 little bottles of gin. It's all a far cry from what I remember as a child, but my Advent calendars were no less exciting. I loved the mystery of the closed doors, the slight crack and crease of the card as you prised one open, the minute picture that was the reward and the excitement of finding tomorrow's number – 'Just to find it, not to open it!' So much anticipation!

Often real doors, rather than cardboard ones, carry the same sense of anticipation and discovery when they're about to open. I can picture the big west door of the church, for example, as I waited behind it, with all my friends and family and my future husband on the other side, and then the music started for me to walk down the aisle. Perhaps you can think of doors that led to interviews and to new jobs, new homes, new friends, new babies; doors where you waited nervously for an exam; doors where you hoped for good news.

Doorways can represent big transitions or just little ones. My daughter, perhaps because of her autism, struggles with any transitions – even between being in bed and out of it or upstairs to downstairs, which can make mornings rather difficult. She finds the liminal space of being neither here nor there very uncomfortable. The word 'liminal' comes from a Latin word meaning 'threshold'. It denotes any narrow space between two wider spaces. Thresholds are spaces to move through, not to stand about in. There's a fine line between anticipation and anxiety.

To get my daughter into school every day, her teacher stands in the doorway and greets her with her first activity – 'Hello! Your question sheet is ready on your desk' – to shorten and ease the transition. Leaving school can be just as difficult, so I do the same thing: waiting on the threshold with the promise of a biscuit generally helps! Strangely, our own doorway at home presents less of a struggle, perhaps because my girl knows that she is entering her safe place again at last after a long day.

Jesus says that he is the door or the gate for the sheep. He stands in that threshold place, in that narrow gap between two wider spaces, like the teacher in the doorway, ready, welcoming and familiar. The sheep can go in and out safely past him, and when they come back from the pasture they recognise their safe place and look forward to home and rest.

Jesus is the door to the biggest transition there is: he says that all who enter through him will be saved. He's the door to salvation and the gate to the kingdom of God. He stands in the transition between life and eternal life, on the threshold that is death, ready to greet us with all that is to come, all his promises of real home and true safety forever.

But Jesus is a door for small transitions as well. He says that the sheep go in and out to pasture through him and that he came to bring life in abundance. He is always there as we move between sleeping and waking, between sickness and health, between sad times and happy times. Today in all your threshold places, as you move between spaces, between activities and between times of day, pause with a brief prayer to acknowledge Jesus the door, as Psalm 121:8 says, 'keep[ing] your going out and your coming in from this time on and forevermore'.

A suggestion

As we stand in the doorway of the new year, make a list of all the threshold spaces you are aware of in your life: small daily ones, larger and more important ones, and transitions that may be on the horizon or hoped for but that haven't happened yet. Looking through your list, consider how Jesus could stand as a door for you in each of those spaces.

A prayer to God the door

Lord, you stand at every threshold. Watch over me as I go out and come in today. Be there in the change from rest to business, from work to home, from conversation to silence, and from the old year to the new: now and every day until at last you open into eternal life.

2 January

Rock

Psalm 18:1–3, 31–33

I love you, O Lord, my strength.
The Lord is my rock, my fortress, and my deliverer,
  my God, my rock in whom I take refuge,
  my shield, and the horn of my salvation, my stronghold.
I call upon the Lord, who is worthy to be praised;
  so I shall be saved from my enemies…
For who is God except the Lord?
  And who is a rock besides our God? –
the God who girded me with strength,
  and made my way safe.
He made my feet like the feet of a deer,
  and set me secure on the heights.

There is a rock in France that I love. It's in the Pyrenees, halfway up a mountain where my family and I used to go to pick blueberries. With our baskets full and our fingers stained purple, my sister and I would go to clamber up Roc de Manoula. It's an easy scramble to the top, where the view of the valley rewards you, dropping away below. I would cling to the top of the rock, enjoying the sensation of the wind, pretending that I was an eagle about to swoop down over the hills or a mountain deer standing sturdily on a peak. On my rock, I could be queen of my castle, a knight protecting a fortress, a battleship crashing through green waves or a solitary saint in perfect touch with nature, like the hermits I'd read about who lived in caves in the cliffs.

All those imaginings are caught up in the images listed by the psalmist here in verse 2. God is a rock, fortress, deliverer, refuge, shield, horn of salvation, stronghold – all in one verse! In this psalm, God the rock offers strength and protection; he is a rock for clinging to and hiding in during times of distress. In verse 33, just after naming God as a rock for the second time, the psalmist writes, 'He made my feet like the feet of a deer, and set me secure on the heights.' God the rock is a dwelling place, a strong foothold, and the psalmist is at home on him, like a mountain deer standing tall and unreachable on a sheer rock face.

In the context of the rest of the psalm, the rock is a martial image: the psalmist is being trained for war and to vanquish enemies. The rock acts as a shield and a fortress, an unassailable place from which arrows can be fired at the enemy. God the rock is a strong position for battle: easy to defend, difficult to attack, standing tall against the onslaught.

In Moses' song, God is a rock because he is reliable and unchangeable: his ways are perfect, he is upright and just (Deuteronomy 32:4). God's righteousness is unassailable, and he cannot be moved. Moses uses the image to point out that God is unlike both the fickle children of Israel, running after idols new and old, and the idols themselves, constantly requiring sacrifices but never acting. God is constant. He can't be coaxed, bribed or swayed, unlike the gods of Israel's enemies: 'Their rock is not like our Rock,' says Moses (Deuteronomy 32:31).

After all those images of strength and solidity, it is all the more surprising that in the hymn 'Lord, enthroned in heavenly splendour', we sing about Jesus as the 'stricken rock with streaming side'. This image comes from 1 Corinthians 10:4, in which Paul identifies Jesus with the rock that Moses struck with his staff in the desert, causing a stream of water to flow for the thirsty Israelites. Paul says, 'For they drank from the spiritual rock that followed them, and the rock was Christ.' The gospel writer John was thinking of the same connection when he made a point of describing the water and blood that flowed together from Jesus' side when he was pierced on the cross.

It's an extraordinary image: the immovable, foundational God the rock, our protection, shield and support, is now vulnerable enough to be struck and wounded, broken open. Yet he still acts as a fortress that we can hide behind, for as our rock and shield, he absorbs that blow for us. And the water that flows as a result is life-giving too.

A question

Read verse 2 again. Which of the list of images of God most resonates with you?

A prayer to God the rock

Lord, you are my strength, my shield, my refuge. You protect me, and you cannot be moved! I stand firm on you and I am safe; I hide in you and cling to you when the storms come. Thank you for the blows you have taken for me, my shield, my refuge, my rock.

3 January

Bird

Deuteronomy 32:10-12

> He sustained him in a desert land,
>   in a howling wilderness waste;
> he shielded him, cared for him,
>   guarded him as the apple of his eye.
> As an eagle stirs up its nest,
>   and hovers over its young;
> as it spreads its wings, takes them up,
>   and bears them aloft on its pinions,
> the Lord alone guided him;
>   no foreign god was with him.

Compared with most twitchers, I'm a beginner at birdwatching. Don't ask me about garden birds – beyond the obvious few, most songbirds, tits and finches look alike to me. I'm better at water birds – I can sort out my gulls from my waders, and from our boat on the Norfolk Broads I love to photograph grey herons, redshanks, avocets and kingfishers. But most thrilling of all is the sight of a marsh harrier soaring above the reeds. I love birds of prey.

I started learning their names early on, when a red kite was still a much more common sight over the fields in France than it was in England. Happily, breeding programmes and conservation have meant that kestrels, buzzards and kites are once again frequently seen in many parts of England, hovering over the fields at the roadside. (If I ever crash my car, it will be because I was trying to identify a bird.) But on holiday in the Pyrenees, the birdwatching is even more exciting – there are vultures and eagles there. One visitor centre even has cameras trained on a rock face so that you can see straight into the nests of huge Griffon vultures and watch them take care of the eggs (only one each) and fledglings. Amazing! I am enraptured by raptors. My family looks on in bemusement.

Bird-spotting in the Bible turns out to be just as exciting. There are sparrows, doves, ravens, owls and eagles, to name only a few. But even more excitingly, if you look closely enough, some of these birds will turn out to be God. Look especially closely at the ones sitting on their nests. Psalms 17, 57 and 91 all contain references to hiding safely under God's wings, protected by God's feathers, like baby birds or eggs beneath their mother. The mother bird is a symbol of God's all-encompassing protection and tenderness. The image is soft where the rock metaphor was hard, but the two pictures both represent a shield, God defending us and hiding us.

In Matthew 23:37, Jesus uses the same image when he laments over Jerusalem: 'How often have I desired to gather your children together as a hen gathers her brood under her wings, and you were not willing!' There is so much heartache and love in such a simple image: God, with a maternal instinct, wants to gather us together, keep us warm and safe.

But there comes a time when the fledgling birds have to fly the nest. The griffon vultures encourage their young to the edge of the cliffs, where they practise flapping their wings and holding them open to feel the warm air rising. Eventually, with a jump, they catch their first ride on a thermal. The parent birds don't abandon them at that point, though; they soar alongside, see them through the more difficult landing and continue to feed them until they are confident to fly independently.

The bird described in today's passage, which could be an eagle or a vulture, is not so much a soft nesting image as a picture of a parent bird pushing its offspring out of the nest. In the same way, says Moses in his song, God guides his people and watches over them even in the hard times of the wilderness, the terrifying and risky time of a first flight. If they fall, we can assume that God, like a mother vulture, will continue to feed them on the ground. There will be a second chance.

When something in life feels as if you are spreading your wings for the first time, jumping from a sheer rock face and hoping for the best, God is a mother vulture: encouraging, protective, fierce and right beside you. Have you ever experienced that warm air rising against your wings? Is there something on the horizon, some small hint of a direction, that little nudge in your spirit? Perhaps it's time to leap off the ledge, knowing that God will soar alongside you. If, however, you have landed on the ground with a bump, don't lose hope. God will continue to feed you where you are while you build up your strength. You will get the chance to have another go at soaring.

A question

Are you being nudged towards a first flight, a risky leap into the unknown? What could that look like for you?

A prayer to God the bird

You spread your wings to shield and cover me, and I am safe and warm under your protection. Although I have been helpless, you have fed me; although I have been flightless, you have patiently nurtured me. Now I need to take my flying lessons from you. Stick close to me, Lord, and show me where to go and what to do.

4 January

Lamb

John 1:26–29

> John answered them, 'I baptise with water. Among you
> stands one whom you do not know, the one who is coming
> after me; I am not worthy to untie the thong of his sandal.'
> This took place in Bethany across the Jordan where John was
> baptising. The next day he saw Jesus coming towards him
> and declared, 'Here is the Lamb of God who takes away the
> sin of the world!'

The old man and the young boy climbed the mountain side by side.
The boy carried the wood for the sacrifice across his back, and every
now and then turned his innocent face up to grin at his father. He was
the only hope of the nations, the promised child, the long-awaited
only son. His father seemed distracted, turning his face away from
the boy's eager looks. The father's heart was breaking. Isaac turned
to him again, this time with a more questioning expression. 'Dad?'

'Here I am, my son.'

'I've got the wood, and you've got the knife and the fire, but haven't
we forgotten something? Where is the lamb for the sacrifice?'

The question hung in the air for a moment. Abraham swallowed
hard. 'God will provide a lamb.'

At the top of the mountain, as the knife was about to plunge down,
the angel's voice sounded at the same time as the bleat from a
nearby thicket. The test was stopped, Abraham was blessed for his

obedience, Isaac was saved and a ram was sacrificed in his place. Not a lamb, a ram. They called the mountain, 'The Lord will provide.'

Isaac's question carried on hanging in the air for nearly 2,000 years. It was hanging there when the Israelites killed lambs and smeared the blood on their doorposts so that the angel of death would pass over their houses the night when all the firstborn died and they were set free from Egypt. Here are our lambs, sacrificed in the place of our sons. Where is the lamb that God will provide?

It was hanging in the air for every lamb and other animal that was sacrificed from then on. Here is a lamb for our sins, and another, and another, and another for the next year's sins. Where is the lamb that God will provide?

It was hanging in the air when Isaiah wrote in chapter 53 about a lamb silent before its shearer and led to slaughter, just after saying that all of us, like sheep, are led astray. Where is the lamb that dies in the place of all these wayward sheep?

Then, some two millennia after Isaac asked it, the question was answered with a shout in the wilderness: 'Look! The Lamb of God who will take away the sins of the world!' (see John 1:29). John the Baptist's answer to Isaac's question echoes back across the years, making sense of the sacrifices, the prophesies, the mourning for cherished sons. Every sacrifice in the past pointed to this one. God's own long-awaited, long-promised son, the only hope of the nations, is the lamb that God will provide.

We have already seen God described as a shepherd. Now Jesus is identified as both the good shepherd and the lamb. Fully shepherd and fully lamb, only he can sing Psalm 23 from both points of view: God walks through the valley of the shadow of death both with us as our shepherd and for us as the lamb. Sometimes, only a metaphor can express such an extraordinary truth.

A suggestion

Spend some time reading the story of Abraham and Isaac (Genesis 22) in your favourite version of the Bible.

A prayer to the lamb of God

Come again, Lamb of God, expected for so long. Come again, Lamb of God, who made an end to all our sins and sacrifices. Come again, Lamb of God, for we are still like sheep that have been led astray. Come, Lamb of God, and bring in that reign of peace when you lie down with the wolf and eat beside the lion and there's no death or killing any more.

5 January

Green shoot

Isaiah 11:1-5, 10

A shoot shall come out from the stock of Jesse,
   and a branch shall grow out of his roots.
The spirit of the Lord shall rest on him,
   the spirit of wisdom and understanding,
   the spirit of counsel and might,
   the spirit of knowledge and the fear of the Lord.
His delight shall be in the fear of the Lord.
He shall not judge by what his eyes see,
   or decide by what his ears hear;
but with righteousness he shall judge the poor,
   and decide with equity for the meek of the earth;
he shall strike the earth with the rod of his mouth,
   and with the breath of his lips he shall kill the wicked.
Righteousness shall be the belt around his waist,
   and faithfulness the belt around his loins...
On that day the root of Jesse shall stand as a signal to the
peoples; the nations shall inquire of him, and his dwelling
shall be glorious.

I think my closest friends all know not to give me houseplants now.
It doesn't matter how closely I follow the advice on the little label
or how easy the plant is supposed to be to care for, it won't last
more than a couple of weeks in my house. And once the plant has
turned brown and lost most of its leaves, I simply pick it up and put
it outside, so my patio looks like an apocalyptic garden centre.

A while ago, though, when I ventured outside, I noticed that a couple of the dry stick plants had started to grow again. The dead parts hadn't revived – they were as brown and shrivelled as before – but from somewhere in the middle of the plant, a new green shoot had started to climb. The new shoots looked nothing like the original plant. Instead of being beautifully shaped and full of leaves, they were long, spindly and ugly, growing at random angles and apparently trying to escape the dry corpse in the pot. But they were there, green shoots growing from what I'd thought was dead wood.

Isaiah predicts the coming of someone who will be like a green shoot growing from the stock of Jesse. This is Jesus' family tree: Jesse is the father of King David. Further back than Jesse is a cast of familiar characters: Ruth and Boaz and their son Obed; Boaz's mother Rahab, who hid the spies in Jericho and joined God's people after the walls fell; all the way back to Abraham and beyond, as Matthew carefully lays out in the beginning of his gospel.

This green shoot is growing from something that looks dead, just a stump in the ground. Matthew lists 28 generations between David and Jesus. The stories that the genealogy brings to mind – Rahab rescuing the spies, Ruth gleaning in the field, the boy king killing the giant – must have already had the flavour of ancient tales. The space between the last page of the Old Testament and the first page of the New represents 400 years of silence. Even as Isaiah was writing this prophecy, 700 years before Christ, the memory of David and Jesse himself was nearly 300 years in the past.

The plant looks dead. It looks as though it has been cut off. But now there's a green shoot, a sign of life. It could become a branch. It offers hope that these times could come again: the times of God being close to his people, of God's power being shown on the earth.

The images that follow in Isaiah 11 speak of peace and power. The Spirit of the Lord will rest on this person, says Isaiah, and he will judge the whole earth with righteousness, and his reign will be so peaceful that a child will be able to lead wolves and leopards and goats and lambs together and the snake won't bite any more. And after this tantalising promise of a return to Eden, Isaiah adds that it will involve every nation and that the shoot of Jesse will stand as a sign to the peoples.

Then, much later, Isaiah goes back to the image of a green shoot, again clearly linking it to the coming Messiah. This time, though, it is a young plant in dry ground, unremarkable, fragile and short-lived. Like the new shoots from my dead plants, 'he had no form or majesty that we should look at him, nothing in his appearance that we should desire him' (53:2). This green shoot is vulnerable: like grass almost everywhere else that it's mentioned in the Bible, it's here today, gone tomorrow, representing mortality.

God the green shoot holds all the hope of new life in tension with the temporary nature of life as we know it on earth. He reminds us that the Word became flesh, and that 'all people are grass' (Isaiah 40:6). God the green shoot offers to share our mortality at the same time as he promises his reign of eternal peace.

A question

Are there areas of your life that seem absolutely dead and finished? What would it look like for a new green shoot to start growing in one of them?

A prayer to the shoot of Jesse

New shoot from the stump of a royal family tree, fresh sign of hope and life to the nations, come as you promised and bring peace. Come as you promised and change our world from the grass that withers and dies into the eternal green of your kingdom.

6 January

Gold, incense and myrrh

Matthew 2:11

> On entering the house, they saw the child with Mary his
> mother; and they knelt down and paid him homage. Then,
> opening their treasure-chests, they offered him gifts of gold,
> frankincense and myrrh.

We all know the picture from countless nativity scenes: the wise men
kneeling and presenting exotic, expensive gifts to the baby Jesus. We
may also know, from many sermons, that there weren't necessarily
three wise men, that they almost certainly didn't turn up at the stable
and that Jesus may have been a toddling two-year-old before they
arrived! Matthew's account is hazy on details that tradition has filled
in, but it is firm on one thing: the gifts that these travellers brought.
Each precious gift was not just costly, but was also a picture, a sort of
concrete prophecy, about who they believed this baby to be. We may
be familiar with the symbolic meaning of each gift from the carol 'We
three kings', but let's look at how they relate to all the images and
metaphors we have explored in this book.

The gift of gold signifies a king or ruler, someone of importance like all
the images of the God in charge, the landowner and master. In those
parables, we saw God as an owner of riches, who entrusts them to us
as stewards and expects to see the return on his investment. As we
saw in the section on God the metalworker, gold can also stand for
purity and perfection. Jesus' reign is absolute, unsullied and eternal.

Incense was used for prayer in the temple, and it signifies holiness.
The rising smoke represented movement between earth and heaven,

like the image of Jesus as the door in the threshold, as well as the literal meaning of the word 'metaphor': God is carried across to us, and our prayers are carried across to heaven. This is a multisensory form of worship: the sight of the rising smoke, heat of the flame and smell of the sweet fragrance are all intended to bring us, body and soul, into God's presence. In fact, this image of holiness is close to the first images we explored, the ones God himself used: fire, a pillar of cloud, the sense of presence in silence.

Myrrh is traditionally explained as being used to anoint a dead body, and therefore as a prophecy of Jesus' significant death. That is true, but myrrh was also used as a medicine and ointment with antiseptic, soothing properties – Mary might have used it on Jesus' nappy rash. If that image made you raise your eyebrows, then you've caught the significance of the myrrh: it's all about the physicality, vulnerability and mortality of the Word made flesh. It represents God really incarnate, really with us, and a human being sharing in every experience of ours.

So at Epiphany, when the church traditionally celebrates the visit of the magi, we have been given a summary of all our metaphors for God. God is holy and huge, unreachable and indefinable, in the incense. God is king and leader, the master of the house entrusting his servants with his riches, in the gold. And, in the myrrh, we find God on earth: God who is bread, a lamb, a bird; God vulnerable and dying; God as Emmanuel; God with us.

A suggestion at the end of week 5

At Epiphany, the day when traditionally the Christmas decorations are packed away for another year, we have a family tradition: we write ourselves little notes and pack them away too. Sometimes they are practical things, such as, 'Amy, you put the tree lights in the plastic box in the garage this year.' Sometimes they are memories of Christmas that might otherwise get lost as we get back into the swing of everyday life. Every Advent, as we unpack the decorations again, we discover last year's notes and remember.

Why not write yourself Epiphany notes to keep inside this book? It could be something that you want to remember: perhaps a metaphor that stood out to you, one of the prayers that resonated with you, something new or interesting that occurred to you while reading. It could be something you would want to remind yourself at the beginning of the book, if you were to read it again. Perhaps something happened in your life over the past five weeks and you want to note how relevant or irrelevant the readings for that day were to you in the light of what was happening. Slip the notes inside the book in the relevant places. Perhaps they will be rediscovered another year.

A prayer

Father, Lord, Holy God,
we have met you in metaphor
and we have glimpsed you in image and experience,
but you are One:
wholly, hugely, indescribably One God,
uncontainable in any of our pictures,
ungraspable in any of our thoughts.
Yet we praise you because we are allowed to know you,
to love you,
to speak with you,
through your Son Jesus Christ,
who came to be with us at Christmas.
He is the image of the invisible God,
now and forever.
Thank you.
Amen

Ideas for group study

Week 1

To begin

Split the group into two, and give both groups two minutes to write down as many words to describe God as they can think of. Stop and compare notes. Do the two groups agree? How big a range of descriptions are there? Do any of the words link to specific stories or passages from the Bible? Do any link directly to someone's experience of God? Which are the most surprising?

Reading

Read the passage about Elijah in its full context (1 Kings 19). Which of the words in the two lists are supported by the descriptions of God in this story? Are any of them contradicted?

For discussion

How do you imagine that Elijah knew that God was not in the earthquake, wind or fire, but discerned him in the silence?

Ask the group to share, in pairs, about a time when they have felt able to discern God's presence.

For prayer

Spend some time, as a group, in silence or with quiet music playing. As a focus, begin with God's question to Elijah: 'What are you doing here?' Finish by singing a short song or saying the Grace together.

For the week ahead

The stories in this chapter vary between surprise encounters with God (such as the burning bush and the angel of the Lord appearing to Gideon) and deliberate meetings with him (Elijah praying for the fire, Moses asking to meet God and Joshua reading from the law). This week, keep a journal of your meetings with God. Plan times when you will stop and pray, but also take note of the times when you feel that God has met you, through people, places, inspirations or ideas.

Week 2

To begin

Invite the group to bring along examples of their own creations – anything from cookery to origami! If anybody really feels that they've never created anything, ask them to bring their favourite work of art. Spend some time looking, listening and learning from each other about the group's creative talents.

Reading

Read the whole of Job 38, the first of several chapters in which God describes his creation to Job. How many artistic disciplines can you find mentioned within the passage? How many separate creations are described? Make a list of each.

For discussion

How do you react to the idea that you are an ongoing creation of God? Can you pinpoint times in your life when some important part of you has been formed or changed?

For prayer

Take two sheets of A4 paper, preferably of two different colours. Cut one of them into strips 2 cm wide down the long side of the paper. Turn the other piece of paper landscape and fold it in half from left to right. Cut, from the folded edge, strips 2 cm apart, stopping 1 cm from the unfolded edge. Then unfold. Give each member of the group one of the long strips and ask them to write (or draw or mark in code) their prayer along it. Pass around the landscape piece, and take it in turns to weave the prayers into it, while praying aloud or quietly with music playing. When all the strips are woven in, hold the finished mat and say a final prayer to offer everyone's prayers to the creator God.

Or: Spread out sheets of paper or a big piece of paper or canvas, and provide coloured pens and any other art materials that work with your group and your space. Read the following poem slowly out loud, twice, leaving space in between for everyone to respond in any way they wish on the paper: with words, drawings and whatever else is available.

Riddle

The word has been spoken, the sower is seed:
The potter becomes the clay.
The tailor is needled and knitted and dyed,
for God becomes flesh today.

The singer is sung, the builder is built,
the weaver is hung on a loom
the blacksmith is heated and beaten and gilt,
for Life becomes lived in the womb.

For the week ahead

Choose one of the artists from the chapter – poet, musician, weaver, potter, clothier, architect, metalworker – and engage in some way with that art this week, whether by researching it, doing it or simply looking out for examples of it. As you do, consider what this might teach you about God the creator.

Week 3

To begin

Most of the parables from this week's collection centre around a
dynamic rather foreign to us today: that of a master or king and his
household of servants. Where, in today's world, can we find a similar
relationship? Do we generally find ourselves in the position of owner
or of servant? How might this affect the way we react to these stories?
Ask everyone in the group to think of one situation in which they are
(or were) closer to the master or owner and one in which they are (or
were) more like the servant, and to bear them both in mind through
the session.

Reading

Read the parable of the unforgiving servant (Matthew 18:23–35).
Do you think the master in this parable acts fairly? Is his reaction
reasonable or does he overreact? Why do you think the servant
demands his small debt so forcibly – what is motivating him? What
has the servant understood (or not understood) about the character
of the master?

For discussion

Many of these parables seem to turn on a servant who underestimates
or misunderstands the character of their master. What does it mean
to be part of God's household? What happens when we have different
ideas about who God is or how he will act? How can we best know
and reflect God's responses to our world?

For prayer

Consider going for a prayer walk around the local area. If that's not
possible, spread out a map of the area or photographs of some of

the different businesses, charities, churches and schools that exist there. Spend some time as a group, in pairs or individually, praying about these specific places and reflecting on how God's household, his kingdom, could respond with regard to each one. Write down any ideas you have in your prayers and discussions, and (if you are using the map or photos) place your thoughts near those places.

For the week ahead

Look at the thoughts and ideas your group had during the prayer time. Think of ways they could be put into action this week, and do something, as a group or as individuals, to act as a member of God's household in your community.

Week 4

To begin

At Christmas we celebrate Emmanuel, God with us. Write some conversation-starter questions on the theme of togetherness on to cards. You could draw one card at a time, inviting answers to the question, or ask everyone to take a card and try to answer it. For a large group, put people in pairs or threes and swap cards every two minutes. Some examples of conversation starters could be:

- Have you ever wanted to be with someone who was miles away?
- Do you think that long-distance relationships can work?
- If you could choose anyone in the world to come and sit next to you right now, who would it be?
- Think of three things you wouldn't want to do alone.
- Do you prefer big crowds, small groups or one other person?
- Do you think that mobile phones and the internet have had a positive or negative effect on loneliness?

Reading

Read John 1:1–18. If possible, find three or four different translations or paraphrases of it. Assign each one to a reader and listen to them, taking it in turns to read a few verses at a time. At the end of the reading, read verses 14 and 18 again. If possible, display those two verses where everyone can see them.

For discussion

How would you put John 1:14 and John 1:18 into your own words? What do they mean to you, or what images and ideas come to mind when you read or hear them?

For prayer

Place images or models of a cross and a manger into the centre of the group as a focus, along with the two verses from John 1 above. Light a candle. Ask everyone to speak the name of a person or situation that needs the presence of God or to think of it silently if they prefer. After a moment of quiet, read verse 14 again slowly. Finish by saying the Grace together.

For the week ahead

Find a way to offer companionship to someone this week, with a visit, a chat at church or a phone call.

Week 5

To begin

Ask everyone to be still and quiet, and set a timer for two minutes. Ask the group to become aware of each of their senses in turn. What can they hear in the background of the quiet room? What do they notice as they look around? What sensations do they feel in their bodies? What are their hands in contact with? Are there tastes or smells to be noticed? When the timer goes, ask everyone what came to their attention for each sense.

Reading

Read Matthew 2:1–12. How many different methods of communication between God and people can you find in this passage?

For discussion

Of all the scriptural metaphors for God in this chapter and in the whole book, which ones have you particularly found yourself returning to? Which ones were surprising? Which ones seemed obvious?

What part do our everyday senses, surroundings and experiences play in how we hear from and communicate with God? How can we use scripture as a guide in these experiences?

For prayer

Make the gifts of the wise men a focus for prayer by gathering a gold object or crown, something scented (such as incense or a scented candle) and something for use on the body (such as soap or hand cream). Ask everyone to think of what they would want to say to Jesus as a king, to Jesus as a huge and holy God and to Jesus as a man among us. The group could speak these three prayers or suggestions for prayers out loud, write them down or pray them silently, with the leader giving space for each one in turn. Finish by reading the following poem, or the prayer from the end of the entry for 6 January.

Hide and seek

Lord whose touch could heal the deaf
and open the eyes of the blind,
you gave us the sense to see you,
you told us to seek and find.

Your poured yourself into a cup of wine,
you broke yourself open in bread.
We hunted for you in the heavens;
you hid yourself here instead.

You are as huge as the rising sun,
as small as the tiniest seed.
We search for you in things we love;
you hide in what we need.

You curled up small in the manger,
you stretched out wide on the tree.
You hid in the face of a stranger,
but you were seeking me:

seeking the long-lost brother,
seeking a lost lamb, too,
and now that we've found each other,
I can be hidden in you.

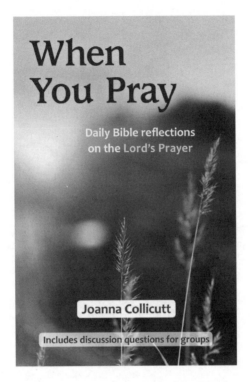

In this updated edition of a classic text, Joanna Collicutt shows how growing as a Christian is rooted in the prayer Jesus gave us. As we pray the Lord's Prayer, we express our relationship with God, absorb gospel values and are also motivated to live them out. As we pray to the Father, in union with the Son, through the power of the Spirit, so we begin to take on the character of Christ.

When You Pray
Daily Bible reflections on the Lord's Prayer
Joanna Collicutt
978 0 85746 867 3 £10.99

brfonline.org.uk

Turned by Divine Love

Starting again with God and with others

JOHN STROYAN

This book, the fruit of prayer, theological reflection and rich human experience, evokes fresh praying and thinking about all the key relationships in our lives, beginning with God. Drawing on the rich Christian traditions of both east and west, it speaks of theology and spirituality, to the head and the heart. It is a book of hope, encouraging us all to make a fresh start with God and, entering more fully into the relationship of love to which he invites us, to go out and to witness to this love. In this unique bringing together of the riches of the Christian east and west is the call to hear God's gracious voice today.

Turned by Divine Love
Starting again with God and with others
John Stroyan
978 0 85746 750 8 £9.99

brfonline.org.uk

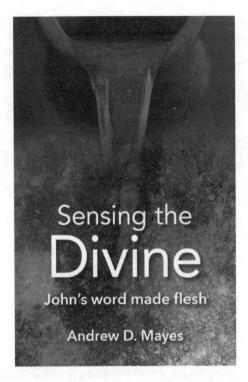

This compelling, inspiring book is an invigorating rereading of the fourth gospel by a well-known spirituality writer who has lived some years in the Holy Land. Uniquely, it approaches John's gospel by exploring how he uses the senses, both physical and spiritual, in his encounter with Jesus Christ, the Word made flesh. This refreshing appreciation of the gospel will activate and stimulate our own discoveries and spiritual quest, not only of the gospel, but also of God's world, ourselves and our mission.

Sensing the Divine
John's word made flesh
Andrew D. Mayes
978 0 85746 658 7 £10.99

brfonline.org.uk

BRF

Transforming
lives and communities

Christian growth and understanding of the Bible

Resourcing individuals, groups and leaders in churches for their
own spiritual journey and for their ministry

Church outreach in the local community

Offering two programmes that churches
are embracing to great effect as they
seek to engage with their local
communities and transform lives

Teaching Christianity in primary schools

Working with children and teachers to explore Christianity
creatively and confidently

Children's and family ministry

Working with churches and families to explore **parenting for faith**
Christianity creatively and bring the Bible alive

Visit **brf.org.uk** for more information on BRF's work

brf.org.uk